An Analysis of

Ludwig Wittgenstein's

Philosophical
Investigations

Michael O'Sullivan

Published by Macat International Ltd
24:13 Coda Centre, 189 Munster Road, London SW6 6AW.

Distributed exclusively by Routledge
2 Park Square, Milton Park, Abingdon, Oxon OX14 4RN
711 Third Avenue, New York, NY 10017, USA

Routledge is an imprint of the Taylor & Francis Group, an informa business

www.macat.com
info@macat.com

Cataloguing in Publication Data
A catalogue record for this book is available from the British Library.
Library of Congress Cataloguing-in-Publication Data is available upon request.
Cover illustration: Etienne Gilfillan

ISBN 978-1-912303-15-1 (hardback)
ISBN 978-1-912127-68-9 (paperback)
ISBN 978-1-912282-03-6 (e-book)

Notice
The information in this book is designed to orientate readers of the work under analysis,
to elucidate and contextualise its key ideas and themes, and to aid in the development
of critical thinking skills. It is not meant to be used, nor should it be used, as a
substitute for original thinking or in place of original writing or research. References and
notes are provided for informational purposes and their presence does not constitute
endorsement of the information or opinions therein. This book is presented solely for
educational purposes. It is sold on the understanding that the publisher is not engaged
to provide any scholarly advice. The publisher has made every effort to ensure that
this book is accurate and up-to-date, but makes no warranties or representations with
regard to the completeness or reliability of the information it contains. The information
and the opinions provided herein are not guaranteed or warranted to produce particular
results and may not be suitable for students of every ability. The publisher shall not be
liable for any loss, damage or disruption arising from any errors or omissions, or from
the use of this book, including, but not limited to, special, incidental, consequential or
other damages caused, or alleged to have been caused, directly or indirectly, by the
information contained within.

CONTENTS

THE MACAT LIBRARY

The Macat Library is a series of unique academic explorations of seminal works in the humanities and social sciences – books and papers that have had a significant and widely recognised impact on their disciplines. It has been created to serve as much more than just a summary of what lies between the covers of a great book. It illuminates and explores the influences on, ideas of, and impact of that book. Our goal is to offer a learning resource that encourages critical thinking and fosters a better, deeper understanding of important ideas.

Each publication is divided into three Sections: Influences, Ideas, and Impact. Each Section has four Modules. These explore every important facet of the work, and the responses to it.

This Section-Module structure makes a Macat Library book easy to use, but it has another important feature. Because each Macat book is written to the same format, it is possible (and encouraged!) to cross-reference multiple Macat books along the same lines of inquiry or research. This allows the reader to open up interesting interdisciplinary pathways.

To further aid your reading, lists of glossary terms and people mentioned are included at the end of this book (these are indicated by an asterisk [*] throughout) – as well as a list of works cited.

Macat has worked with the University of Cambridge to identify the elements of critical thinking and understand the ways in which six different skills combine to enable effective thinking.
Three allow us to fully understand a problem; three more give us the tools to solve it. Together, these six skills make up the **PACIER** model of critical thinking. They are:

ANALYSIS – understanding how an argument is built
EVALUATION – exploring the strengths and weaknesses of an argument
INTERPRETATION – understanding issues of meaning

CREATIVE THINKING – coming up with new ideas and fresh connections
PROBLEM-SOLVING – producing strong solutions
REASONING – creating strong arguments

To find out more, visit **WWW.MACAT.COM.**

CRITICAL THINKING AND
PHILOSOPHICAL INVESTIGATIONS

Primary critical thinking skill: ANALYSIS
Secondary critical thinking skill: INTERPRETATION

Many still consider Ludwig Wittgenstein's 1953 *Philosophical Investigations* to be one of the breakthrough works of twentieth-century philosophy.

The book sets out a radically new conception of philosophy itself, and demonstrates all the attributes of a fine analytical mind. Taking an argument from Plato and subjecting it to detailed (and very clear) analysis, Wittgenstein shows his understanding of how the sequence and function of differing parts of a highly-complex argument can be broken down and assessed. In so doing, he reaches a logical position of simultaneous agreement and disagreement with Plato's philosophical position.

Philosophical Investigations is also a powerful example of the skill of interpretation. Philosophical problems often arise from confusions in the use of language – and the way to solve these problems, Wittgenstein posits, is by clarifying language use. He argues that philosophers must study ordinary uses of language and examine how people use it as a tool in their everyday lives. In this highly-interpretative way, the meaning of a word or sentence becomes relative to the context (people, culture, community) in which it is used. Rather than debate abstract problems, Wittgenstein urges philosophers to concern themselves with ordinary life and the concrete situations in which humans find themselves.

ABOUT THE AUTHOR OF THE ORIGINAL WORK

Austrian philosopher **Ludwig Wittgenstein** was born into a hugely wealthy Viennese family in 1889. Originally destined to be an engineer, he became interested in the philosophy of mathematics and then philosophy generally while a student at Manchester University in England. Wittgenstein fought in the Austrian Army in World War I and wrote his first important work while a soldier. He gave up philosophy for a while, but returned to it and eventually taught at Cambridge University. He died, after a battle with cancer, in 1951.

ABOUT THE AUTHOR OF THE ANALYSIS

Dr Michael O'Sullivan is a tutor in the Department of Philosophy, King's College London. He is the editor of *Wittgenstein and Perception*.

ABOUT MACAT

GREAT WORKS FOR CRITICAL THINKING

Macat is focused on making the ideas of the world's great thinkers accessible and comprehensible to everybody, everywhere, in ways that promote the development of enhanced critical thinking skills.

It works with leading academics from the world's top universities to produce new analyses that focus on the ideas and the impact of the most influential works ever written across a wide variety of academic disciplines. Each of the works that sit at the heart of its growing library is an enduring example of great thinking. But by setting them in context – and looking at the influences that shaped their authors, as well as the responses they provoked – Macat encourages readers to look at these classics and game-changers with fresh eyes. Readers learn to think, engage and challenge their ideas, rather than simply accepting them.

'Macat offers an amazing first-of-its-kind tool for interdisciplinary learning and research. Its focus on works that transformed their disciplines and its rigorous approach, drawing on the world's leading experts and educational institutions, opens up a world-class education to anyone.'

Andreas Schleicher,
Director for Education and Skills, Organisation for Economic
Co-operation and Development

'Macat is taking on some of the major challenges in university education ... They have drawn together a strong team of active academics who are producing teaching materials that are novel in the breadth of their approach.'

Prof Lord Broers,
former Vice-Chancellor of the University of Cambridge

'The Macat vision is exceptionally exciting. It focuses upon new modes of learning which analyse and explain seminal texts which have profoundly influenced world thinking and so social and economic development. It promotes the kind of critical thinking which is essential for any society and economy. This is the learning of the future.'

Rt Hon Charles Clarke, former UK Secretary of State for Education

'The Macat analyses provide immediate access to the critical conversation surrounding the books that have shaped their respective discipline, which will make them an invaluable resource to all of those, students and teachers, working in the field.'

Professor William Tronzo, University of California at San Diego

WAYS IN TO THE TEXT

KEY POINTS

- Ludwig Wittgenstein (1889–1951) was an Austrian philosopher who became one of the most important thinkers of the twentieth century.

- Published in 1953, *Philosophical Investigations* discusses language, the human mind, and the nature of philosophy itself.

- *Philosophical Investigations* is *the* major statement of Wittgenstein's later philosophical work and one of the most important and influential books ever written on the philosophy of language and the philosophy of mind.

Who was Ludwig Wittgenstein?

Ludwig Wittgenstein was born in Vienna, Austria in 1889. As a young man he studied engineering, but his mathematical work in this area led him to developing an interest in the philosophy of mathematics and then philosophy in general.* Wittgenstein read and admired the philosopher Bertrand Russell's* book, *The Principles of Mathematics*. In 1911, he went to England to study with Russell at the University of Cambridge, but left to fight for Austria in World War I.* During the war he wrote a philosophical book, the *Tractatus Logico-Philosophicus,*[1] which became very influential. The work focused on showing how language and the world relate to each other, explaining how our words and sentences acquire meaning. Believing he had now solved philosophy's main problems, Wittgenstein gave up philosophy and became a schoolteacher in Austria.

In 1929, Wittgenstein returned to Cambridge to teach and began a new phase in his philosophical thinking. There he argued against many of the things he once believed, including what he had written in the *Tractatus*. He now thought that the *Tractatus* account of language was too far removed from our everyday experience of using language.

Wittgenstein did not, however, publish his new ideas during his lifetime. Instead he discussed them with friends and students. He wrote many sets of notes and drafts for a book setting out his ideas, though he was never quite happy with what he had written. His students compiled and edited the material included in *Philosophical Investigations*, publishing the book after his death in 1951.

Investigations, like the *Tractatus*, gave rise to new schools of thought in philosophy. Wittgenstein is now widely regarded as one of the greatest thinkers of the twentieth century, and many people see *Philosophical Investigations* as his best work.

What Does *Philosophical Investigations* Say?

Published in 1953, Ludwig Wittgenstein's *Philosophical Investigations* is a complex work. In it, Wittgenstein does not focus on a single argument, but instead develops a number of themes, the most important of which is about language. He believes that philosophical problems arise from the confused use of language and that the way to solve those problems is by clarifying language use—not by discovering new facts or inventing new theories.

Investigations provides an alternative to conventional ways of thinking about philosophy. Philosophers often view themselves as producing general theories about the world. Wittgenstein argues that this is a mistake. He also challenges the popular belief at the time that he wrote *Investigations* that science can solve all important intellectual problems. To him, philosophical problems are quite different from scientific ones and cannot be solved by finding out more about the world.

If we want to understand both language and mind, Wittgenstein thinks we must study ordinary uses of language. We must look at how people use language in their everyday lives. This will differ greatly in different societies and cultures. So when Wittgenstein asks: what is the meaning of a word or sentence? He answers: the meaning lies in the way it is used in language. In other words, to understand meaning, we should look at how different people, cultures, and communities use words and sentences because meaning is essentially a public and social phenomenon.

Wittgenstein criticizes the idea that the German mathematician and philosopher Gottlob Frege,* among others, proposed: that meanings are abstract. Wittgenstein contended instead that the needs of everyday life determine the way we use words and sentences. We use language to make jokes, buy food, or play games, he says. Abstract rules do not govern the way we use language, and the way people have used language in the past does not tell us how to use words now.

Wittgenstein argues, too, that private language*—language that can only one person can understand—is impossible. So language cannot take its meaning from a particular individual's inner thoughts because meanings are not private mental states. Language depends on public use to have meaning.

Investigations moves away from the abstract and highlights the importance of human context. Wittgenstein argues that the problems of philosophy cannot be understood independently of the human situations in which they arise. In order to understand abstract philosophical ideas like truth and meaning, we need to look at how human beings actually live their lives.

The book is still very widely studied and discussed. It is certainly one of the most influential philosophical works of the twentieth century. However, few people would say that it has been entirely understood. Interpreters still argue about what it means, while philosophers and other readers continue to find new insights and ideas in it.

Why Does *Philosophical Investigations* Matter?

Philosophical Investigations is a difficult work to understand, partly because it deals with difficult and complex questions. But Wittgenstein also writes in an unusual way. Rather than putting forward the themes of the book in a straightforward argument, he offers remarks on and illustrates those themes. As a result, even though individual sections are often easy to read, it becomes hard to see how they all fit together.

Nevertheless, *Investigations* can still be pleasurable to read. Wittgenstein writes well, so the book can be enjoyed on a literary level. It is full of interesting ideas, metaphors, and suggestions. His idea of comparing the ways that we use language to the playing of games, for example, has had an impact on many readers. They have found that the book inspires them to think in new ways. Wittgenstein himself says in the preface that his aim is to stimulate readers to develop thoughts of their own.

The book is relevant to many different disciplines. It is certainly a revolutionary work of philosophy, but it has also had an impact on a number of other areas. Its emphasis on how social environment shapes language was important to linguists. In addition, Wittgenstein's thoughts on how we use language to do things other than to state truths has influenced both theologians* and literary critics. For example, theologians are interested in how religious language not only states supposed facts about God, but also expresses emotions.

Philosophical Investigations has also had an effect outside academia, inspiring writers, poets, and film-makers, including I. A. Richards,* Derek Jarman,* and David Foster Wallace.* That is because Wittgenstein emphasizes the importance of everyday life and language and the differences between societies and cultures. This still matters today when we are much more aware of the importance of cultural differences than writers had been before Wittgenstein's time.

The book also offers a method from which readers can learn. Wittgenstein approaches difficult problems by finding new ways to look at them. He believes that the best way to solve a problem is to formulate it correctly. Often, once we know what questions to ask, then it becomes easier to find the solution. Suppose, for example, that we ask for the meaning of the word "please." We would go wrong if we looked for a single meaning that the word stands for. Instead we should look to how it is used. We say "please" in order to acquire something, to be polite, and so on.

Wittgenstein thinks philosophical problems come about because of the way we use language. So if we clarify the words and sentences that we use, we will come to see the world much more clearly. Wittgenstein believes that philosophical problems are essentially linguistic confusions. It is a controversial view. To what extent are philosophical problems really a language issue? But, whatever the case, Wittgenstein's method of approaching problems by examining the ways in which we describe them is useful.

NOTES

1   Ludwig Wittgenstein, *Tractatus Logico-Philosophicus*, trans. D. F. Pears and B. F. McGuinness (London: Routledge, 1962).

SECTION 1
INFLUENCES

THE AUTHOR AND THE HISTORICAL CONTEXT

KEY POINTS

- *Philosophical Investigations* is one of the most important works of philosophy written in the twentieth century. It has influenced the way we think about language, the mind, and philosophy itself.

- Wittgenstein knew some of the most important contemporary thinkers in Britain and Germany. While he took account of their work, he was also a fiercely independent thinker who subjected others' views and his own to intense scrutiny.

- Wittgenstein wrote two great works of philosophy: the *Tractatus Logico-Philosophicus* and *Philosophical Investigations*. *Investigations* makes profound criticisms of the thinking in the *Tractatus.*

Why Read This Text?

Published in 1953, *Philosophical Investigations* is one of the most important philosophical works of the twentieth century and the final, authoritative statement of Ludwig Wittgenstein's thought. In his youth, Wittgenstein had put forward bold and original philosophical ideas in his book, the *Tractatus Logico-Philosophicus*. However, when he was older, he changed his opinions radically, and he suggests in *Investigations* a very different approach to philosophy.

Wittgenstein introduces in the book a range of central philosophical issues concerning language, the human mind, and the nature of philosophy itself. His views on each of these topics have been

> 66 The figure of Ludwig Wittgenstein exerts a very special fascination that is not wholly explained by the enormous influence he has had on the development of philosophy this century. Even those quite unconcerned with analytical philosophy find him compelling. Poems have been written about him, paintings inspired by him, his work has been set to music. 99
>
> Ray Monk, *Ludwig Wittgenstein: the Duty of Genius*

discussed ever since. In each case, he proposes that we pay close attention to the actual situations in which human beings find themselves, and he emphasizes careful attention to detail rather than the formulation of grand theories. Instead of inventing a theory to show how some words become the names of objects, he says, we should look at how names are *actually used* in everyday speech.

Wittgenstein's approach to the philosophy of language and mind has been influential. But so has his attitude to philosophy itself. Wittgenstein sees philosophical problems as a result of confused or ill–understood uses of language and believes the way to solve these problems is to clarify how language is used.

Author's Life

Ludwig Wittgenstein was born in Austria in 1889 into a family of extremely wealthy Viennese industrialists. It was a highly cultured and, in particular, musical family. His brother, Paul Wittgenstein, was a successful concert pianist, and several other members of the family were musically talented. Wittgenstein himself was musically gifted, although his tastes were conservative. He had a passion for the classical German and Austrian tradition of Mozart,* Beethoven,* and Schubert* and a disdain for the music of his own day.[1]

Following his father's wishes, Wittgenstein studied engineering at the University of Manchester in England and while there he became interested in logic and the philosophy of mathematics. In 1911, he left Manchester without taking his degree to study at the University of Cambridge with Bertrand Russell,* the eminent philosopher and logician (someone who studies logic*). Russell had written an important book about the foundations of mathematics, *The Principles of Mathematics*,[2] which Wittgenstein had read and admired.

Wittgenstein left Cambridge at the outbreak of World War I* and joined the Austrian army. While a soldier, he wrote his early masterpiece, the *Tractatus Logico-Philosophicus*. First published in 1921, the *Tractatus* gives a general theory of language, showing how words and sentences acquire their meaning. Wittgenstein believed that philosophical questions arose from problems about meaning and language, and the *Tractatus* showed how to solve such problems. In that work, he thought he had solved the main problems of philosophy, so he gave up philosophy and became a schoolteacher in Austria.

In the meantime, the *Tractatus* became enormously influential both in England and in Europe. By the time Wittgenstein returned to Cambridge in 1929, he had gained a great reputation as an original thinker prepared to challenge accepted beliefs. However, he had changed his own views radically since writing the *Tractacus*. While nobody knows for sure, that may have been the reason he returned to philosophy and Cambridge—he believed that he had work left to do. At Cambridge, his lectures and philosophical discussions on logic and the philosophy of language, mind, and mathematics attracted many students, eager to understand and develop his ideas. During his life, Wittgenstein's thoughts spread by word of mouth and the informal circulation of lecture notes and manuscripts. These notes and manuscripts were to form the basis of the *Investigations*.

Wittgenstein worked as a teacher and scholar at the University of Cambridge from 1929 until his death in 1951 at the age of 62. He developed most of the ideas behind the *Investigations* there and also wrote parts of the book during extended stays in isolated parts of Norway and Ireland.[3] He produced most of the text in its current form between about 1936 and 1949.

Author's Background

When Wittgenstein was young, Vienna was a place of great cultural creativity. The psychoanalytical theories of Sigmund Freud* (treating emotional and mental problems by having a patient talk about dreams, feelings, and memories),* the music of Arnold Schoenberg,* and the art of Gustav Klimt* all emerged in that city in the early twentieth century. Although Wittgenstein disliked modernist* music that broke with previous traditions, he was nevertheless influenced by the innovative cultural environment in Vienna and maintained a strong interest in Freud's theories. His one architectural work, a house on the Kundmanngasse in Vienna that he designed for his sister, shows modernist influences.

In the preface to *Philosophical Investigations*, Wittgenstein writes of the "darkness of this time."[4] Since he was writing in January 1945, many readers have assumed that he was referring to World War II*. However, biographer Ray Monk has argued that Wittgenstein was actually referring to the cultural environment of the time—in particular, the dominance of the natural sciences.[5] Although Wittgenstein was familiar with and interested in science, by the time he wrote *Investigations*, he had come to think that its intellectual importance was dangerously exaggerated. His later work can be seen as an early reaction against what is today sometimes called "scientism":* the view that science is the only important way of understanding the world.

NOTES

1   Ray Monk, *Ludwig Wittgenstein: the Duty of Genius* (London: Vintage, 1991), 13.

2   Bertrand Russell, *The Principles of Mathematics* (London: Allen and Unwin, 1903).

3   Monk, Ludwig Wittgenstein, 361ff and 520ff.

4   Ludwig Wittgenstein, *Philosophical Investigations*, trans. Elizabeth Anscombe (Oxford: Blackwell, 2001).

5   Monk, *Ludwig Wittgenstein*, 486.

MODULE 2
ACADEMIC CONTEXT

KEY POINTS

- Many modern philosophers, especially since Immanuel Kant,* were concerned with understanding the scope and nature of human thought.

- In the early twentieth century, philosophers such as Gottlob Frege* and Bertrand Russell* came to believe that the best way to study human thought was to study language.

- Wittgenstein agreed with Frege and Russell on the importance of language, but he emphasized the many different uses to which it can be put.

The Work In Its Context

In the late eighteenth century, the great German philosopher Immanuel Kant introduced a new approach to philosophy that remained influential into the twentieth century and beyond. Kant looked at philosophical problems by asking how the structure of the human mind and human thought affect our knowledge of the world. He believed that studying the ways in which we think about the world can throw light on the traditional philosophical questions about truth, meaning, and knowledge.

Kant called this approach the "Copernican turn." The great mathematician and astronomer, Copernicus,* had revolutionized Renaissance* thought in the early sixteenth century by reversing the usual view of the solar system. Instead of the established view that the sun revolved around the earth, he said that the earth revolved around the sun. Similarly, Kant believed, we could explain human knowledge by assuming it was shaped by the structure of the human mind, rather

> ❝ Only with Frege was the proper object of philosophy finally established: namely, first, that the goal of philosophy is the analysis of the structure of *thought*; secondly, that the study of thought is to be sharply distinguished from the study of the psychological processes of *thinking*; and, finally, that the only proper method for analysing thought consists in the analysis of *language*. ❞
>
> Michael Dummett, *Truth and Other Enigmas*

than just the structure of the world around us.

Kant's project was to understand the limits of human knowledge and reason, because then we could know why some of the central philosophical questions had never been answered. Such questions included whether God exists and whether the universe is eternal. They cannot be answered, Kant thought, because they attempt the impossible: to respond to questions beyond the limits of human reason.

Overview of the Field

In the twentieth century, philosophers put Kant's question in a linguistic form. They saw a direct link between the limits of thought and the limits of language, of what can be expressed in words. They therefore came to see language as central to philosophy.

When Wittgenstein wrote *Investigations*, the development of what is often called "analytical philosophy,"* had revolutionized philosophy in the English-speaking world. That strand of philosophy focused on logic,* careful attention to language, and a respect for science.

A central figure in this development was the German philosopher and mathematician Gottlob Frege, who published his *Foundations of Arithmetic* in 1884.[1] Frege made an enormous contribution to the philosophy of language. He aimed to analyze thought by examining the language in which thought is expressed. But, unlike Wittgenstein, his analysis was geared towards scientific and mathematical uses of language.

Another key figure was Wittgenstein's mentor, Bertrand Russell, the British philosopher and logician.* Russell saw language's main purpose as giving an accurate representation of the world. He thought that if language could be made more accurate and precise, the representation of the world would be better too. He used the tools of modern logic* to achieve this aim. Russell expressed these views in influential works including the article "On Denoting,"[2] and his great multi-volume work of mathematical logic, co-authored with Alfred North Whitehead,* *Principia Mathematica*.[3]

Academic Influences

It is difficult to know specifically which philosophers had an impact on Wittgenstein, as he generally does not cite authors or give conventional references. But he does mention Gottlob Frege as a crucially important influence. One way to understand *Investigations* is as a modification of Frege's own philosophy, extending the focus on language to non-scientific uses.

During Wittgenstein's early years at the University of Cambridge (1911–14), Russell was his teacher. Wittgenstein also came to have an acknowledged influence on Russell. However, by 1936, when Wittgenstein began to write *Investigations*, the two philosophers were no longer close friends and had little personal contact. Wittgenstein disliked the popular, non-technical works that Russell was writing by that time. Russell, in turn, disliked Wittgenstein's later work, but he was still an important influence on his student. The difference between the two men was that Russell thought the aim of language was the representation of reality—forming a sort of picture of the world—whereas Wittgenstein stressed the many different purposes for which language can be used. And where Russell thought that language had to be refined and made more precise, Wittgenstein insisted that ordinary language is adequate as it is.

In many respects, *Investigations* runs directly counter to the most important movement in the philosophical scene of the 1930s, one that Frege, Russell, and the early Wittgenstein himself greatly influenced: logical positivism.* A group of Austrian and German philosophers known as the "Vienna Circle," the most important of whom was Rudolph Carnap,* had developed the movement, which emphasized the logical analysis of language. They were empiricists,* people who believe all human knowledge comes from experience. Their view was that only sentences that could be empirically verified—confirmed by experiment or observation—had meaning.

So, for example, it would be meaning*ful* to ask what time it is in Japan, because that can be checked. But it is meaning*less* to ask whether God is good, or whether Mozart or Beethoven is the better composer, because (the logical positivists thought) such things cannot be confirmed or denied. On that basis, they criticized much of traditional philosophical, ethical, religious, and artistic conversation as meaningless.

Wittgenstein disagreed. He thought that the scientific use of language is only one use among others, so in fact there could be no general way of deciding what was meaningful, as the logical positivists thought.

NOTES

1 Gottlob Frege, *Foundatons of Arithmetic*, trans. J. L. Austin (Oxford: Blackwell, 1950).

2 Bertrand Russell, "On Denoting," *Mind* 14 (1905): 479–93.

3 A. N. Whitehead and Bertrand Russell, *Principia Mathematica* (Cambridge: Cambridge University Press, 1910–13).

MODULE 3
THE PROBLEM

KEY POINTS

- Philosophers were interested in the question: how do words and sentences get their meaning?

- Gottlob Frege* had understood meaning in terms of truth: the meaning of a sentence, he thought, is given by the conditions under which it is true. The logical positivists* thought that the meaning of a sentence is given by the way we decide whether it is true or false.

- Wittgenstein rejected the idea that there is a single way of analyzing language. He said we should look at the ways language is used to understand its nature.

Core Question

Ludwig Wittgenstein never gives us a clear statement of his intentions in writing *Philosophical Investigations*, so it is difficult to identify the core question that it is designed to answer. One useful way of approaching the book, however, is to think of it as addressing the question: how do our words and sentences get their meanings? That question was crucial, too, to the philosophers who had come just before Wittgenstein.

However, the book also addresses a broader question: how do our mental states—our beliefs, desires, expectations, memories, and so on—get their meanings? In this second question, the word "meaning" must have a different (though related) sense. This question concerns what philosophers call the "intentionality"* of these mental states, or how they are directed at things. How, for example, does a desire come to be a desire *for* a particular thing? How does my desire for ice cream come to be a desire specifically for ice cream?

> **❝** The aims of this school [logical analysis] are less spectacular than those of most philosophers in the past, but some of its achievements are as solid as those of the men of science. **❞**
>
> Bertrand Russell, *History of Western Philosophy*

These are perhaps the most-fundamental questions that can be asked about language and the mind. They have come to be particularly urgent in modern times because of the success of natural science. For instance, scientists can explain more and more of the world in terms, for instance, of animal behavior. Human behavior, however, is less easily explained scientifically, precisely because so much of it involves meanings and intentions. So, the nature of meaning becomes a pressing intellectual question.

The Participants

Wittgenstein's most important philosophical influence, Gottlob Frege, had concentrated on formulating a semantic* theory—that is, a theory of the meaning of language. He argued that the "unit of meaning" is the thought, and that the meaning of a thought lies in its "truth condition," or the way the world has to be for the thought to be true.

Bertrand Russell* took up Frege's ideas in *The Philosophy of Logical Atomism*, a book[1] based on lectures that he delivered in 1918. In that work, Russell explains how our talk and thought about the world acquires meaning. According to him, we are able to think about the world because our mental states represent states of affairs in the world (representationalism).* This representational relation between mental states and real states of affairs is the starting point: it explains the various types of thought we can have about the world. So, if I say, "The cat is on the chair," I am giving a representation of the world. If the cat *is* on the chair, what I say is true. If it isn't, what I say is false. Either way, I have represented the cat as being on the chair.

Wittgenstein also agreed with this viewpoint in the *Tractacus Logico-Philosophicus*, but he later came to believe that this is only one way to use language among many others. So, if I say, "I'm tired," I may merely be telling you how I'm feeling. But I may also be trying to get you to make the tea so I can put my feet up. In that case, the real reason that I say, "I'm tired," is not in order to represent the world at all, but to influence your actions.

Russell believed that we could discover how our thoughts hook on to the world by analyzing them into their constituent parts (logical atomism).* If we do this, we discover that these constituent parts are private perceptions and experiences—what Russell called "sense data."* Ultimately, it is only sense data that we can name as constituent parts, as it is only with sense data that we ever have direct perceptual contact.

When Wittgenstein was developing the ideas of *Philosophical Investigations* in the 1930s and 1940s, the most vigorous philosophical movement of the era, logical positivism*, was increasingly dominating the philosophical debate. Like Frege and Russell, the logical positivists focused on linguistic meaning. They believed that the role of philosophy was to discover the correct analysis of sentences and thereby discover their true meaning. Indeed, that was the only way to assess whether they were meaningful at all.

The logical positivists put forward a theory that only sentences that can be empirically* verified—confirmed by experiment or observation—count as meaningful. So, for example, abstract, religious, or metaphysical* (what there fundamentally *is*) discussion is literally meaningless. Take a sentence like, "There is a daisy growing on top of Kilimanjaro." You can check whether that is true or not by looking for a daisy growing on top of Kilimanjaro. But it is not possible to check whether a sentence like, "God loves us," is true. Therefore, according to the logical positivists, it has no meaning whatsoever.

The Contemporary Debate

In *Investigations*, Wittgenstein rejects many of the ideas of Frege, Russell and the logical positivists. He rarely cites other philosophers by name, though Frege and Russell (his former teacher) are among the few exceptions. In key passages of the *Investigations*, Wittgenstein is clearly responding to Russell, even where he does not mention him by name.[2]

Wittgenstein says we should focus on the uses of language rather than on words and sentences that are divorced from their contexts. He encourages us to examine "language games:" particular, concrete situations where people use language for specific purposes. Those encompass the scientific uses of language that Frege and the logical positivists concentrated on. More controversially, Wittgenstein also includes literary and religious uses of language, which the positivists had condemned as meaningless.

Wittgenstein rejects the idea that there is a general rule for understanding meaning and such a thing as a single correct analysis of a sentence. He believes that we can analyze thoughts in different ways, depending on their purpose.

For example, we might explain the sentence, "John is a bachelor," by saying, "John is not married." But the second sentence is neither more basic nor more fundamental than the first. It is simply more useful for the purpose of explaining the sentence to someone who does not understand the word "bachelor." The logical positivist idea that philosophy acts as an aid to scientific work by clarifying the real meaning of sentences cannot be maintained.

Or think again of the sentence, "I'm tired." It might be a dispassionate report of how I'm feeling, or it might be an attempt to get you to make the tea. Two utterly different things, but the sentence is the same. The important point is: I'm using the same sentence for different purposes on two different occasions. Since meaning, for late Wittgenstein, is use, it's not sentences that have meaning, but the particular circumstances in which they are said. Suppose I say, "God loves us." I might be reporting on the way I take God to be, or trying to cheer you up, or making a joke. These are all utterly different uses of the same sentence. You can't ask whether the sentence is meaningful or not. So, according to Wittgenstein, it follows that logical positivism is false.

Wittgenstein dismisses Russell's ideas wholesale, particularly the abstract notion of "representation." Instead, he says, we should look to our specific aims and purposes in concrete situations if we want to understand our thoughts and talk about the world. The meaning of language comes from a shared, public environment, not from personal experience. Wittgenstein therefore rejects Russell's concept of "sense data," too.

Although Wittgenstein denounced the ideas of his predecessors, he understood profoundly their arguments. He had absorbed the genuine lessons of modern logic* and modern philosophy and, as a result, *Philosophical Investigations* was regarded as a powerful attack on his fellow philosophers.

NOTES

1   Bertrand Russell, *The Philosophy of Logical Atomism* (London: Routledge, 2009).

2   For example, § (Remark) 79 clearly alludes to Russell's theory of descriptions, and the discussions of private language and inner experience beginning around § (Remark) 243 engage with Russell's views on perception.

3   Frederick Douglass, introduction to *Narrative of the Life of Frederick Douglass: an American Slave*, ed. Benjamin Quarles (Cambridge, MA: Harvard University Press, 1988).

MODULE 4
THE AUTHOR'S CONTRIBUTION

KEY POINTS

- Wittgenstein summarized his view in the slogan "meaning is use."

- Wittgenstein's view placed a new emphasis on the analysis of ordinary uses of language and the role that language plays in everyday life.

- In the work of his predecessors, and even in Wittgenstein's own earlier work, *scientific* uses of language were often emphasized as particularly important. In *Philosophical Investigations*, Wittgenstein sees science as just one use of language among many others.

Author's Aims

Ludwig Wittgenstein once described his aim as getting people "to change their style of thinking."[1] His purpose in *Philosophical Investigations* is not so much to convince people of specific philosophical guiding principles as to uncover the roots of common mistakes and confusions. In particular, Wittgenstein wants to lead us away from broad, general theories about language and the mind and encourage us instead to pay attention to particulars.[2] In philosophy, unlike physics and biology, there is no need to form these general theories, Wittgenstein says, because the subject is difficult to understand. Rather, our ordinary ways of thinking and talking about the world are fine as they are. Philosophical problems arise only when we misuse the tools we already have at our disposal. Taking it to an extreme, if Wittgenstein's aims were successful, the problems would disappear and the philosophers would just have to keep quiet.

> **❝** For a large class of cases—though not for all—in which we employ the word 'meaning' it can be defined thus: the meaning of a word is its use in the language. **❞**
>
> Ludwig Wittgenstein, *Philosophical Investigations*

Some commentators[3] believe that Wittgenstein thought the aims of philosophy should be to prevent bad thinking, not to arrive at truths. They say he practiced philosophy as a kind of therapy, aiming simply to remove intellectual problems and confusions. *Philosophical Investigations* does, however, contain many insights into the traditional problems of the philosophy of language, the philosophy of mind, and the philosophy of mathematics. Its approach is certainly against coming up with theories, but it also makes a contribution to positive philosophical thought.

Wittgenstein's aims influenced the way he wrote. His tone is conversational and it does not have the structure of a conventional written argument. Voices appear, representing the sort of philosophical approaches that Wittgenstein wants to challenge, and then he responds in his own voice. This unusual structure makes it difficult to interpret Wittgenstein's intentions. As a result, contemporary debate on the book focuses not only on the arguments, but also on how best to understand what Wittgenstein hoped to achieve with it.

Approach

Wittgenstein's approach to language emphasizes the specific uses that speakers give to words and sentences. In order to understand how language works, he invented the idea of a "language game."* A language game is a simple situation in which language is used for a particular purpose. The moves in the game are the words of the speakers. As in a game of chess, definite rules govern those moves.

For example, at the beginning of *Investigations*, Wittgenstein describes a language game played by people building a house. A builder calls out words like "slab," "pillar," and so on, and an assistant fetches the appropriate item. Wittgenstein's thought is that if we ask what words like "slab" *mean* for builders, we must describe what they *do* with these words.

Wittgenstein believed a speaker of a language like English plays many different language games and that the use of a given word will depend on the particular situation. There are no definite rules governing the use of the language as a whole, only within specific situations. So, to understand what speakers of the language are doing on a particular occasion, we need to understand which language game they are playing.

One result of this approach is that, for Wittgenstein, the scientist is merely playing one language game among many. Scientific usage has no special status in understanding language use as a whole, and Wittgenstein placed far less emphasis on scientific usage than his predecessors.

Contribution In Context

Although Wittgenstein criticized the views of fellow philosophers Gottlob Frege* and Bertrand Russell,* he also learned a great deal from them. One way of looking at his work is that he deepened and extended their insights. They concentrated on the use of scientific language, and Wittgenstein broadened the debate to cover other things that we do with language.

One can find some parallels with Wittgenstein's criticisms of this earlier school of philosophical thought in other writings of the period. There are some similarities, for example, with the "ordinary language philosophers,"* who were based largely at the University of Oxford. One was J. L. Austin,* who also believed that philosophy should clear up linguistic confusions and that language is best understood by examining how ordinary speakers use words. The philosopher Gilbert Ryle,* like Austin and Wittgenstein, made a careful examination of language use. He also shared with Wittgenstein an emphasis on the importance of behavior. If we want to understand the nature of mental states such as anger, we should look at the ways in which angry people behave.

But while Ryle was sympathetic to Wittgenstein's ideas, Austin at first couldn't understand them. Perhaps that was because of the unconventional way in which they were presented: not as a traditional academic argument, but as a series of remarks, illustrations, and examples. In general, Wittgenstein's critical response to logical positivism,* with its logic-based analysis of language, and mainstream analytical philosophy* was more radical and challenging than that of other critics, including Austin and Ryle. That meant it took much longer for Wittgenstein's work to be accepted into the academic mainstream.

NOTES

1   Ludwig Wittgenstein, *Lectures and Conversations* (Oxford: Blackwell, 1967) §
    (Remark) 28.

2   Ludwig Wittgenstein, *Philosophical Investigations*, trans. Elizabeth Anscombe
    (Oxford: Blackwell, 2001) (Remark) 109.

3   See in particular the essays in Rupert Read and Alice Crary, eds., *The New
    Wittgenstein* (London: Routledge, 2000).

SECTION 2
IDEAS

MODULE 5
MAIN IDEAS

KEY POINTS

- According to *Philosophical Investigations*, the meaning of a word lies in how it is used in language. So, in order to understand the meanings of words and sentences, we need to look at the specific situations in which they are used.

- The understanding of language depends on objects and behavior that are observable by at least some people. The meanings of words cannot depend on purely private sensations.

- The ideas are not presented as a single flowing argument. Instead Wittgenstein makes a large number of interrelated remarks, showing the many connections between the themes he discusses.

Key Themes

Wittgenstein's *Philosophical Investigations* contains several main themes. The first is the idea that *meaning* is best understood in terms of *use*. The second is about his discussion of rules and how they are followed. The third concerns argument against "private language"*—a language understood by only one person.

The book begins with Wittgenstein's views about language and meaning,[1] where he puts forward his idea that the meaning of an expression comes from its use in human life. "For a *large* class of cases—though not for all—in which we employ the word 'meaning,'" he writes, "it can be defined thus: the meaning of a word is its use in the language."[2] In particular, he attacks the idea that names of things and people get their meaning simply by being attached to individual

> 66 The best that I could write would never be more than philosophical remarks; my thoughts were soon crippled if I tried to force them on in any single direction against their natural inclination. And this was, of course, connected with the very nature of the investigation. For this compels us to travel over a wide field of thought criss-cross in every direction. The philosophical remarks in this book are, as it were, a number of sketches of landscapes which were made in the course of these long and involved journeyings. 99
>
> Ludwig Wittgenstein, *Philosophical Investigations*

things.

Wittgenstein then discusses following rules.[3] Here he argues that following a particular rule (for example, a rule about the correct use of a word i.e. that "bachelor" applies only to unmarried adult males) is not just about interpreting a particular word correctly. Instead, he says that following rules is about reaching agreement with others on how we are to speak and act.

Next comes the "private language argument."[4] Wittgenstein argues that words for mental states such as "pain" do not get their meaning from being associated with the personal—meaning private— experiences of the speaker. These are experiences that only the speaker knows. Instead, like other terms, words like "pain" get their meaning from communication with others and from public use.

Exploring The Ideas

Wittgenstein points to language's broad range of uses. He argues that we can only understand speech and behavior by referring to people's specific aims and the particular circumstances of their lives. Language use is part of what Wittgenstein calls a "form of life."[5]

Languages like English and French do not merely function to communicate thoughts. They also express the attitudes and ways of life of English and French speakers. Take expressions like, "Thank God," or "for the greater glory of God." Someone who uses these expressions is expressing a certain attitude to life. If a listener does not understand these expressions, we cannot explain them merely by telling them who God is. It may be that their culture is so different that they cannot understand the *attitude* that is being expressed.

Wittgenstein says that if the lion could speak, we would not understand him.[6] Why not? It is not that we and the lion would not talk about the same things. Most likely, we would both have words for antelopes and mountains. But that wouldn't be enough for understanding to take place, because the lion's way of life and outlook on the world would be significantly different. In short, we have different forms of life.

Wittgenstein believed we need to look at the particular circumstances in which language is used. He calls these "language games,"* in which words and sentences are used according to certain rules and for particular purposes.

He argues that we can only understand the difference between correct and incorrect uses of words and sentences by looking at language games. This does, however, lead to the question: what governs the correctness or incorrectness of future uses of language?

Wittgenstein argues that nothing in the past use of any word or expression is strong enough to determine how it will be used in the future. There are always different ways of interpreting past use to fit with new uses.

In general, no rules concerning the use of words are sufficiently strong that they can determine what counts as "correct" use in new circumstances. Rules can always be re-interpreted, so different future behaviors can be described in a way that makes them fit with any existing rule. Wittgenstein writes, "No course of action could be determined by a rule, because every course of action can be made out to accord with the rule."[7] When situations change, very often we need to make new decisions about how to use language.

Wittgenstein applies the same conclusion to private mental entities*—ideas, thoughts, feelings—as he does to abstract rules: that they do not govern language use. Mental representations can be thought of as rules that are spelled out in the mind rather than on paper, and like such rules, they can be re-interpreted to fit with different sorts of future applications.

More generally, Wittgenstein argues against the idea that any language could take its meaning from the private mental life of the individual. We are tempted to think that the language we use to describe feelings and sensations is personal. For example, the word "pain" as *I* use it gets its meaning from *my* private sensation of pain. But Wittgenstein argues that no word could work like this. The correctness and incorrectness of words must have public standards against which they are measured and cannot depend on private experience.* If they did, there would be no way of checking whether they were being used correctly or incorrectly.

Language And Expression

Philosophical Investigations is a beautifully written work that has a great deal of literary merit. Its language is not overly formal, is understandable and is largely free of technical terminology. As a result, it can be a very enjoyable book to read.

However, that does not mean it is easy to understand. This is partly because Wittgenstein doesn't state his ideas and arguments clearly. Instead, he allows them to grow out of a wide-ranging discussion that covers many areas. In his preface, he writes that the nature of his investigation means that the reader must "travel over a wide field of thought criss-cross in every direction."[8]

The result is that the book is difficult to place in conventional academic philosophy. Different readers can interpret it differently, and it can be very hard to see just how Wittgenstein's ideas line up with those of other philosophers.

There are two distinct views on Wittgenstein's writing style. Some commentators—for example, Michael Dummett, the British philosopher,*—suggest that the book's style is the result of Wittgenstein's personality, rather than its philosophical content. They reason that Wittgenstein's views could have been expressed in a more conventional philosophical form, backed up by clear and explicit arguments.[9] Others, such as American philosopher Stanley Cavell,* argue that the style of *Investigations* is essential to its message.[1010] Part of Wittgenstein's point, Cavell says, is that the attempt to formulate general theories leads to mistakes and confusion, and that we can only come to a clear view of language by careful consideration of specific cases.

NOTES

1   Ludwig Wittgenstein, *Philosophical Investigations*, trans. Elizabeth Anscombe (Oxford: Blackwell, 2001), §§ (Remarks) 1–184.

2   Wittgenstein, *Philosophical Investigations*, (Remark) 43.

3   Wittgenstein, *Philosophical Investigations,* (Remarks) 185–242.

4   Wittgenstein, *Philosophical Investigations*, (Remarks) 243–363.

5   Wittgenstein, *Philosophical Investigations*, (Remarks) 19, 241.

6   Wittgenstein, *Philosophical Investigations*, (Remarks) 223.

7   Wittgenstein, *Philosophical Investigations*, (Remarks) 202.

8   Wittgenstein, *Philosophical Investigations*, vii.

9   See, for example, Michael Dummett, "Wittgenstein's Philosophy of Mathematics," in *Truth and Other Enigmas* (London: Duckworth, 1978).

10 Stanley Cavell, *The Claim of Reason* (Oxford: Oxford University Press, 1979, xx.

6   Du Bois, *The Souls of Black Folk*, 10–11.

7   Du Bois, *The Souls of Black Folk*, 10.

MODULE 6
SECONDARY IDEAS

KEY POINTS

- Wittgenstein believes that philosophy should not attempt to gain new knowledge. Instead, it should solve misconceptions that arise from confusions in our thought.

- "Aspect perception"* means experiences in which we can hear or see things in different ways. Wittgenstein uses such experiences to discuss the relationship between perception and thought.

- Wittgenstein's views have been widely studied, but philosophers have not yet accepted all of his ideas.

Other Ideas

Philosophical Investigations is a broad-ranging book that touches on many topics. It contains several subsidiary themes: Ludwig Wittgenstein's understanding of philosophy; his critique of conceptual analysis* (the analysis of words and concepts to discover their meaning), and the notion of what is called "aspect perception"* (how the same object can be seen in different ways). This can also be thought of as "seeing as."

In the book, Wittgenstein says, "Philosophical problems arise when language goes on holiday."[1] His idea is that philosophical confusions occur when we use language in unsuitable ways. It is not that there is anything wrong with a particular word or phrase when it is used in its original, natural way. It goes wrong when it is applied outside its normal context. He imagines someone asking, "What time is it on the sun?"[2] This question has no definitive answer, but not because there is anything vague or unclear about asking for the time in normal

> **❝ What is your aim in philosophy? To shew [show] the fly the way out of the fly-bottle. ❞**
> Ludwig Wittgenstein, *Philosophical Investigations*

circumstances.

The method of conceptual analysis had been important to Wittgenstein's immediate philosophical predecessors, such as Bertrand Russell* and the logical positivists.* Conceptual analysis involved studying language by looking at words and sentences to analyze their real meaning. Wittgenstein argues that this method is flawed: there is no such thing as a single correct analysis of a given sentence.

The second part of the book focuses on the philosophy of psychology,* although Wittgenstein did not review this part for publication. Some commentators, including the British philosopher Peter Hacker,* argue that it should not be considered part of *Investigations* at all. The best-known passages look at aspect perception—a type of experience that the Gestalt school* of psychologists studied, in which, for example, one sees two different figures in the same shape—as it pertains to the relationship between perception and thought.

Wittgenstein uses the example of a diagram that can be seen either as a picture of a duck or a picture of a rabbit. If you look at the diagram for a long time, it seems to switch repeatedly between being a duck-picture and a rabbit-picture. Such "aspect switches" are interesting because they can be interpreted either as seeing something new or as having a new thought, so that thought and perception seem to overlap. "Hence the flashing of an aspect on us," Wittgenstein writes, "seems half visual experience, half thought."[3]

Exploring The Ideas

Wittgenstein presents his negative critique of conceptual analysis clearly and without room for doubt. This is one of the points in the book in which a reader can identify an explicit argument. However, his attack on the conception of analysis is very specific to Russell, who saw the analysis of concepts as the main point of philosophy. This makes understanding Wittgenstein's point difficult for readers who are not familiar with Russell's writings.

Wittgenstein gives his views of this method, but he also presents an alternative by introducing language games:* imagined scenarios in which people use language for specific purposes that differ from, but also throw light on, our own. The focus changes from words and sentences to specific utterances and uses of language.

Picture two people in different countries where it's raining. Both make the comment "It's raining." It's the same sentence but it is also two different utterances that could have been said for different reasons. One person might have been telling someone to take an umbrella; the other might have been making idle conversation. Wittgenstein's point is that the specific context creates the meaning.

Wittgenstein does not give the language-game method an explicit definition. Instead he gives many examples of language games. He urges us, "Don't think, but look!"[4] Here Wittgenstein's literary abilities are put to good use and he describes his scenarios vividly. He presents, for example, a community where the language consists of the use of words like "slab" and "pillar," and he imagines how different the life is in that community.[5] He displays a striking imaginative skill in conceiving it, so many readers who are not familiar with philosophical methods have nevertheless intuitively grasped the language-game method in *Investigations*.

In his discussions on aspect perception, Wittgenstein returns again and again to the problem of whether an aspect experience is a matter of seeing or of thinking. It seems to have features of both. On the one hand, it looks as though the interpretation of the duck/rabbit as a duck is akin to having a thought. On the other hand, the fact that it is a visual interpretation means it is more like *seeing* a new object, or seeing the same object in a new way.

While opinions differ on how these examples relate to the other themes of *Investigations*, Wittgenstein does draw one explicit parallel: just as with pictures for a person viewing them, the way in which words and sentences are understood depends on the background and point of view of the person who hears them. A speaker of English, for example, has a different response depending on whether the word "bank" is used to refer to a financial institution or to the bank of a river.

Overlooked

Vast amounts have now been published about Wittgenstein's *Philosophical Investigations*. It is unlikely that many sections of the text, or aspects of its argument, have been entirely overlooked. Still, it is possible to identify certain features that have been relatively neglected and may yet prove to be of lasting philosophical significance.

Although Wittgenstein's philosophy of language has been studied extensively, certain elements have still not been entirely explored. One interesting question is what lessons Wittgenstein's approach for contemporary philosophy of language and linguistic theory might hold. Most important is the role of context in understanding. Speakers of a language rely on contextual factors, as well as knowledge of the language, to understand each other. Crucially important to our mutual understanding is the fact that we live distinctly human lives: "If a lion could talk," Wittgenstein writes, "we could not understand him."[6]

Scholars may have overlooked this point in the past because some influential interpretations of Wittgenstein's views on language make them seem out-dated. In particular, the American philosopher John Searle* considered Wittgenstein to be a descriptivist when it came to proper names—in other words, that Wittgenstein believed that the meaning of a name could be identified by a cluster of descriptions.[7]

For example, the meaning of the name "Moses" might be identified with such descriptions as "the man who led the Israelites out of Egypt." This view has become unpopular in recent philosophy, particularly since the publication of *Naming and Necessity* by Saul Kripke,*[8] an American philosopher and logician However, it is quite possible to argue that Wittgenstein was *not* a descriptivist in this sense, simply because he was against all general theories.

NOTES

1   Ludwig Wittgenstein, *Philosophical Investigations*, trans. Elizabeth Anscombe (Oxford: Blackwell, 2001), (Remark) 38.

2   Wittgenstein, *Philosophical Investigations,* (Remark) 350.

3   Wittgenstein, *Philosophical Investigations*, 168.

4   Wittgenstein, *Philosophical Investigations*, (Remark) 66.

5   Wittgenstein, *Philosophical Investigations*, (Remark) 6.

6   Wittgenstein, *Philosophical Investigations*, 190.

7   John Searle, "Proper names," *Mind* 67 (1958) 166–73.

8   Saul Kripke, *Naming and Necessity* (Oxford: Blackwell, 1980).

MODULE 7
ACHIEVEMENT

KEY POINTS

- Wittgenstein inspired a new way of thinking about philosophy and the relationship between philosophy and science.

- In recent decades, there has been a return to metaphysics*—what makes up reality—and theorizing about the nature of the world in philosophy. As a result, Wittgenstein's influence has declined.

- Wittgenstein's ideas have been influential in many disciplines other than philosophy.

Assessing The Argument

Ludwig Wittgenstein inspired new ways of thinking both about philosophy itself and the relationship between philosophy and science. His conception of philosophy continues to be influential today. According to Wittgenstein, philosophy is not about formulating general theories about the world. Instead, its aim should be to clear up conceptual confusions.

His views on the difference between science and philosophy have also been influential. He believes that the two have quite different purposes. The aim of science is to gain new knowledge of the world and explain it by formulating theories. Philosophy, by contrast, contributes not knowledge but understanding. Through philosophical discussion, we come to a better understanding of our own thoughts and ideas.

Some commentators, perhaps most prominently the American philosopher Richard Rorty,* have argued that Wittgenstein has

> 66 A picture held us captive. And we could not get outside it, for it lay in our language and language seemed to repeat it to us inexorably. 99
>
> Ludwig Wittgenstein, *Philosophical Investigations*

shown that philosophy has come to an end.[1] It is no longer an intellectual discipline, insofar as its aim was to increase our knowledge of the world, and science can now perform this function. And although philosophy has aspired to discuss deeper questions concerning goodness or the meaning of life, it has been superseded by imaginative literature. This school of thought is based on a controversial reading of Wittgenstein's arguments *against* explanatory theories in philosophy.

Achievement In Context

Within the philosophical community no consensus has formed about the value and significance of *Philosophical Investigations*. Some philosophers believe the book has radical lessons for philosophy that have still not been fully accepted or understood.[2] They cite, in particular, Wittgenstein's argument that the careful investigation of language shows that traditional philosophical investigations into the metaphysical* nature of the world (the fundamental elements of reality) are based on confusions. Others view the work as dogmatic and unconvincing.[3] They continue to pursue traditional philosophical questions that Wittgenstein believed to be senseless or misleading.

It is probably true that *Investigations* is today less influential than it was in the 1950s and 1960s. Metaphysics—the branch of philosophy that deals with the fundamental things that make up reality—is once again popular under the influence of philosophers such as Saul Kripke* and David Lewis,* and that philosophical approach goes against the spirit of *Investigations*. Wittgenstein's view of philosophy— one concerned with our ways of conceiving of the world—has been replaced by theorizing about the nature of the world itself. Many analytical philosophers* do not take questions of language to be as central to philosophy as their predecessors in the middle of the twentieth century. It remains to be seen, however, whether this is a temporary trend or a permanent state of affairs.

Wittgenstein's early influence was mostly restricted to Britain and North America. Several of his students became academics in British and American universities and introduced serious discussion of his work there.[4] However, even on the European Continent, let alone the rest of the world, Wittgenstein's work was associated with the narrow field of English-speaking analytical philosophy. This has changed in recent years, with the work of philosophers such as Jacques Bouveresse* and Alain Badiou* in France, along with a new interest in exploring connections between the work of Wittgenstein and his German contemporary Martin Heidegger.*[5]

Limitations

Wittgenstein's work has had an impact across the humanities and social sciences, not just in philosophy. One field in which his influence has been particularly notable is theology.* As a result of the concepts in *Philosophical Investigations*, some theologians have moved away from thinking of religion as a metaphysical doctrine (a set of ideas that are taught or are believed to be true) or a theory about the origin or nature of the world.[6] Their focus has changed from religious doctrine to religious practice—what actually happens in a religion. More accurately, Wittgensteinian theologians insist that religious doctrines should be interpreted within the context of religious practice. Fundamentally, this is an argument about how religious language should be understood, and they apply Wittgenstein's notion that meaning is use: if we wish to understand the meaning of religious terms, we must look at how they are used.

Some authors, most prominently the Canadian philosopher Kai

Nielsen,* characterized the Wittgensteinian view of religion as "fideism."* Fideism is the view that religious belief is or should be based on faith rather than reason. However, Wittgensteinian religious thinkers, such as D. Z. Phillips,* have disputed that characterization as a misinterpretation.[7] Wittgenstein does not hold that religious beliefs cannot be criticized on philosophical or scientific grounds.

Sociology* and anthropology* are other areas where Wittgenstein has had an influence—in particular, his emphasis that the world view of the subject is what is important, with its aim of describing a situation from the subject's point of view and in terms of his or her own practices.

A notable example is the subfield of sociology of science. A prominent recent trend in this area is to look at different scientific viewpoints from their own point of view. According to this approach, shifts from one scientific viewpoint to another are not explained as progressive moves towards what the theorist knows to be the truth. Instead, we should understand the work of past scientists in *their* own terms, using the concepts that they themselves used. An early enthusiast for this approach was Thomas Kuhn,* whose *Structure of Scientific Revolutions* explicitly acknowledges Wittgenstein's influence.[8] A more recent example is the work of David Bloor,* author of *Wittgenstein, Rules and Institutions.*[9]

Wittgenstein has had an influence in a range of other disciplines, including literary criticism, art history, and education.[10] These applications stray quite far from the topics that Wittgenstein explicitly discusses in *Philosophical Investigations*—so much so that it is impossible to say whether he would have approved of them.

NOTES

1   Richard Rorty, *Philosophy and the Mirror of Nature* (Princeton, NJ: Princeton University Press, 1979).

2   For recent examples, see Paul Horwich, *Wittgenstein's Metaphilosophy* (Oxford: Oxford University Press, 2013) and Charles Travis, *Thought's Footing* (Oxford: Oxford University Press, 2006).

3   See, for example, Timothy Williamson, *The Philosophy of Philosophy* (Oxford: Blackwell, 2007).

4   Important examples are Norman Malcolm at Cornell, Elizabeth Anscombe at Oxford and Peter Geach at Birmingham and Leeds.

5   See for example Lee Braver, *Groundless Grounds: a Study of Wittgenstein and Heidegger* (Cambridge, Mass.: MIT Press, 2012).

6   See for example Fergus Kerr, *Theology after Wittgenstein* (Oxford: Blackwell, 1986).

7   Kai Nielsen and D. Z. Phillips, *Wittgensteinian Fideism?* (London: SCM Press, 2005).

8   Thomas Kuhn, *The Structure of Scientific Revolutions* (Chicago: University of Chicago Press, 1962).

9   David Bloor, *Wittgenstein, Rules and Institutions* (London: Routledge, 1997).

10 See, for example, James Guetti, *Wittgenstein and the Grammar of Literary Experience* (Athens GA: University of Georgia Press, 1993).

PLACE IN THE AUTHOR'S WORK

KEY POINTS

- Wittgenstein was concerned throughout his career with the relationship between language and thought.

- *Philosophical Investigations* was the major statement of his later philosophy, and it contrasts with his early work, the *Tractatus Logico-Philosophicus*.

- *Tractatus* and *Philosophical Investigations* are Wittgenstein's most famous and widely studied works, but the latter has probably exerted the greatest influence on subsequent thinkers.

Positioning

Ludwig Wittgenstein's philosophical career divides naturally into two main periods. From 1911 to 1914 he worked on philosophy at the University of Cambridge. *Tractatus Logico-Philosophicus*,[1] the short book he wrote while fighting in World War I* and as a prisoner of war in Monte Cassino in Italy at the end of the war, expressed his early philosophical views. He then gave up philosophy and worked as a schoolteacher in rural Austria, before returning in 1929 to Cambridge to study philosophy again and begin a new period that lasted until his death.

Philosophical Investigations is the central work of Wittgenstein's mature period. It is the culmination of his research between 1929 and 1949. Other manuscripts and sets of remarks from the 1930s have been published, and they show how Wittgenstein's thought developed, culminating in the ideas that appear in *Investigations*.[2]

Wittgenstein's students edited and published *Philosophical*

> 66 Four years ago I had occasion to re-read my first
> book (the *Tractatus Logico-Philosophicus*) and to explain
> its ideas to someone. It suddenly seemed to me that I
> should publish those old thoughts and the new ones
> together: that the latter could be seen in the right light
> only by contrast with and against the background of my
> old ways of thinking. 99
>
> Ludwig Wittgenstein, *Philosophical Investigations*

Investigations after his death. Although he prepared most of the manuscript in its current form, it is impossible to say whether he would have made further changes before publication. Scholars also disagree about whether the section generally known as "Part Two" of *Investigations* should be regarded as part of the book or as a separate work.[3]

Wittgenstein continued to write on philosophical matters in the few years between the completion of the *Investigations* and his death in 1951. Although he did not produce any more book-length works, several of his typescripts from this period have since been published, organized according to subject matter. Two major themes were the philosophy of psychology (writings on this topic were published under the title *Remarks on the Philosophy of Psychology*)[4] and the theory of knowledge (*On Certainty*).[5]

These works broadly continue the direction of *Investigations*, though they are sufficiently distinctive that some commentators have coined the term "third Wittgenstein" to describe them.[6] In *On Certainty* in particular, Wittgenstein deals with the problem of skepticism,* the view that genuine knowledge of the world is impossible. This problem had dominated much of philosophical thought since the seventeenth century, but it is largely absent from *Investigations*.

Integration

Throughout his career, Wittgenstein was interested in certain broad topics. He sought to understand the relationship between language, thought, and the world. He wanted to explain how our words and sentences get their meaning and how they succeed in being *about* things in the world.

Nevertheless, Wittgenstein's later writings contrast sharply with his earlier ones, both in style and content. The contrast is such that commentators sometimes speak as if there were two Wittgensteins.[7] The *Tractatus* is written in a highly compressed and somber way and has a complex structure. The style of *Investigations* is far more conversational, and it can appear quite formless—it consists of a long series of short and somewhat loosely related remarks. On closer investigation, this assumption turns out to be misleading: the book has a carefully planned structure.

The philosophical positions of the two periods are also very different. In fact, in some ways, *Investigations* argues the opposite of the *Tractatus's* position. In his preface, Wittgenstein suggests that his new work can "be seen in the right light only by contrast with and against the background of my old way of thinking."[8]

The *Tractatus* presented an abstract conception of language inspired by logic.* It saw the main function of language as the representation of the world, and it put forward a "picture theory." According to that theory, sentences "pictured" reality, and the meaning of a given sentence was how it pictured the world. In contrast, *Investigations* emphasizes the importance of ordinary human life in determining the meanings of the words and sentences that we use. It sees representation as only one function of language among many, and it concentrates instead on the use of words and sentences in specific situations.

Significance

Unsurprisingly, Wittgenstein's initial influence also came in two waves.

The *Tractatus* was enormously influential in the 1920s and 1930s, as can be seen in the works of Bertrand Russell* and other English philosophers such as Frank Ramsey.* Moreover, it was extremely important in the philosophy of logical positivism.*

So Wittgenstein was already famous within the philosophical community when he returned to philosophy in 1929 and began the reconsideration of his philosophical position that was to culminate in *Investigations*. His new work aroused great curiosity among readers of philosophy, but since he published very little, at first his ideas spread mostly by word of mouth.

Investigations became part of a movement away from logical positivism. It influenced the "ordinary language philosophy"* of the 1950s, with its emphasis on careful attention to language use. But it is too quirky a work to fit neatly into any one category. It also influenced developments in the philosophy of mind and language, the philosophy of science, and many other areas—particularly in the first few decades after Wittgenstein's death.

Most commentators would agree that, for better or worse, Wittgenstein's impact has waned somewhat in recent decades.[9] Although some philosophers today would call themselves "Wittgensteinians," they are fewer in number than in the past. Nevertheless, his ideas are an important part of the background of modern philosophy, and *Philosophical Investigations* is probably his most enduringly influential work.

NOTES

1   Ludwig Wittgenstein *Tractatus Logico-Philosophicus*, trans. D. F. Pears and B. F. McGuinness (London: Routledge and Kegan Paul, 1962).

2   The most important of these manuscripts have been published as Ludwig Wittgenstein, *Philosophical Remarks*, ed. Rush Rhees, trans. Raymond Hargreaves and Roger White (Oxford: Blackwell, 1975); Ludwig Wittgenstein, *The Blue and Brown Books* (Oxford: Blackwell, 1958) and Ludwig Wittgenstein *Philosophical Grammar*, ed. Rush Rhees, trans. Anthony Kenny (Oxford: Blackwell, 1974).

3   Notably, it is treated as such in the fourth edition of the book, edited by
     Peter Hacker and Joachim Schulte (Oxford: Blackwell, 2009).

4   Ludwig Wittgenstein, *Remarks on the Philosophy of Psychology*, trans.
     G. E. M. Anscombe, vol. 1 (Oxford: Blackwell, 1980) and *Remarks on the
     Philosophy of Psychology*, trans. C. G. Luckhardt and M. A. E. Aue, vol. 2
     (Oxford: Blackwell, 1980).

5   Ludwig Wittgenstein, *On Certainty*, trans. Denis Paul and G. E. M.
     Anscombe (Oxford: Blackwell, 1969).

6   See Daniele Moyal-Sharrock ed., *The Third Wittgenstein* (Aldershot:
     Ashgate, 2004).

7   Influential proponents of the "two Wittgensteins" view include David Pears,
     Wittgenstein (London: Fontana, 1971), and Peter Hacker, *Insight and
     Illusion* (Oxford: Clarendon Press, 1972).

8   Ludwig Wittgenstein, *Philosophical Investigations*, trans. Elizabeth
     Anscombe (Oxford: Blackwell, 2001), vii.

9   For a recent discussion, see Peter Hacker, *Connections and Controversies*
     (Oxford: Oxford University Press, 2013), xvii.

SECTION 3
IMPACT

MODULE 9
THE FIRST RESPONSES

KEY POINTS

- People criticized Wittgenstein for abandoning the work of philosophy as it was traditionally understood.

- *Philosophical Investigations* was published after Wittgenstein's death, and while he was still alive, he rarely responded directly to criticisms.

- At first, Wittgenstein's ideas were not published in articles or books, but circulated through conversations and informal notes. A group of admirers who heard about his views in this informal way shaped the early reception of his ideas.

Criticism

Philosophical Investigations was not published until 1953, two years after Ludwig Wittgenstein's death. During his lifetime, only a small number of scholars who were his own students had access to the text. They were deeply sympathetic to his project, and it was only after *Investigations* was published in full that substantive criticism and debate began as critics started to study and evaluate Wittgenstein's arguments in detail.

Some more traditionally minded philosophers thought Wittgenstein's later work proposed abandoning the traditionally accepted task of philosophy: to contribute to the advancement of our knowledge of the world. Bertrand Russell,* who admired and influenced Wittgenstein's early work, thought his later ideas were an attempt to avoid the hard theoretical work of the discipline.[1] He was also disturbed by Wittgenstein's apparent move away from the uniting of philosophy with science. Russell had always thought that philosophy

> // The earlier Wittgenstein was a man addicted to passionately intense thinking, profoundly aware of difficult problems of which I, like him, felt the importance, and possessed (or at least so I thought) of true philosophical genius. The later Wittgenstein, on the contrary, seems to have grown tired of serious thinking, and to have invented a doctrine which would make such an activity unnecessary. //
>
> Bertrand Russell, *My Philosophical Development*

ought to be in partnership with science, with philosophers and scientists engaged in a common activity. That idea seemed incompatible with Wittgenstein's new thinking.

Similarly, the young Austrian philosopher Karl Popper* believed that Wittgenstein's new ideas trivialized philosophy.[2] According to Popper, philosophy deals with genuine intellectual problems about the nature of the world, just as science does. But he thought Wittgenstein no longer saw philosophy as solving problems, but instead merely as completing puzzles and trivial confusions arising from our thought and talk about the world. Wittgensteinian philosophy, Popper believed, had turned away from investigating the real world in favor of merely investigating language.

Responses

Since *Philosophical Investigations* was published after his death, Wittgenstein never had the opportunity to respond to critics of the completed work. Even before publication, although he was active as a teacher at the University of Cambridge, Wittgenstein wrote in isolation and did not often discuss his work as it developed. Unlike most academics, he did not present his work-in-progress to professional colleagues or at conferences. Nor, with one exception[3]—the article,

"Some Remarks on Logical Form"—did he publish articles in academic journals.

Instead, the task of defending and developing Wittgenstein's ideas fell to a new generation of philosophers who were profoundly influenced by his thought. Many of these philosophers had been his students at Cambridge University or knew him personally there. Wittgenstein named some of them—Elizabeth Anscombe,* Rush Rhees,* and G. H. von Wright*—as his literary administrators, responsible for the preparation of *Investigations* for publication. The work of philosophers Norman Malcolm* and Peter Geach,* who was also a student of Wittgenstein, shows his profound influence.

One important point that these thinkers made was that Wittgensteinian methods and ideas could be usefully applied to traditional philosophical concerns. They addressed issues that Wittgenstein had never grappled with himself and, in doing so, showed that Wittgenstein's influence could actually be seen as enriching the philosophical tradition rather than undermining it.

Elizabeth Anscombe, for example, wrote important work on the philosophy of action and ethics* where Wittgenstein's influence was apparent. Particularly noteworthy were her book *Intention*[4] and her article "Modern Moral Philosophy."[5] Peter Geach's book, *Mental Acts,*[6] brought a Wittgensteinian perspective to the philosophy of mind. And Norman Malcolm addressed issues in epistemology* (the theory of knowledge), including the problem of skepticism.*[7]

Conflict And Consensus

In the decades since the publication of *Philosophical Investigations*, those for and against Wittgenstein's ideas have engaged in a lively debate about a number of key issues. One concerns the nature of philosophy and its relation to science. Philosophical naturalists*—who say that science and philosophy should comprise a single intellectual enterprise, and that philosophical problems can and should be tackled using the methods of science—oppose Wittgenstein views and those of his supporters. Many metaphysical* philosophers also believe, in contrast to Wittgenstein, that part of the role of philosophy is to construct explanatory theories of the world.

A second area of debate focuses on the philosophy of language. Wittgensteinians have criticized the theory that evaluates the meanings of sentences in a language like English in terms of the conditions under which the sentence counts as true. They believe that what is important in determining meaning is not so much the truth conditions of a sentence, but rather the uses to which the sentences are put.

The third area of debate involves the philosophy of mind. Wittgensteinians and their opponents have disagreed about whether we can meaningfully speak of private experiences.* Private experiences, if they exist, are feelings or sensations that belong only to a particular individual and that cannot be adequately described in language or be known or understood by others.

Philosophers are still arguing about all these issues, and Wittgenstein's followers continue to contribute to the debates.

NOTES

1   Bertrand Russell, *My Philosophical Development* (London: Allen and Unwin, 1959), 216–7.

2   Karl Popper, *Conjectures and Refutations* (London: Routledge, 2002), 92–3.

3   Ludwig Wittgenstein, "Some Remarks on Logical Form," *Proceedings of the Aristotelian Society*, Supplementary Volume 9 (1929): 162–71.

4   Elizabeth Anscombe, *Intention* (Oxford: Blackwell, 1958).

5   Elizabeth Anscombe, "Modern Moral Philosophy," *Philosophy* 33 (1958): 1–19.

6   Peter Geach, *Mental Acts: Their Content and their Objects* (London: Routledge, 1957).

7   Norman Malcolm, *Dreaming* (London: Routledge, 1967).

6   Du Bois, *The Souls of Black Folk*, 221–234.

7   W. E. B. Du Bois, *Dusk of Dawn: Essay Towards an Autobiography of a Race* (New York: Harcourt Brace, 1940), 76.

MODULE 10
THE EVOLVING DEBATE

KEY POINTS

- *Philosophical Investigations* encouraged a focus in the philosophy of language on the different ways in which language can be used in practical, everyday situations.

- The work gave rise to a school of Wittgensteinian thinkers. They applied Wittgenstein's methods and ideas to areas of philosophy that Wittgenstein himself never covered in detail, including ethics, the philosophy of religion, and many areas of the theory of knowledge.

- Contemporary thinkers are still using Wittgensteinian methods and ideas to explore language and the mind.

Uses And Problems

Wittgenstein introduced a new emphasis on ordinary language and the use of linguistic expressions in specific situations. Previous philosophers of language, such as Gottlob Frege,* had often written as if meaning were based in the expressions of the language itself, divorced from the circumstances in which it was used.

Many contemporary philosophers believe in the possibility of constructing a theory of meaning for language. Such a theory would tell us how *facts* about the meanings of expressions in a language determine what speakers mean. Major figures such as Donald Davidson,* Michael Dummett,* and David Kaplan* have supported this approach.

Simply put, the Wittgensteinian challenge to this idea stems from the vital importance of context in understanding utterances. What speakers know merely by virtue of knowing a language is not a strong

> 66 What we are supplying are really remarks on the natural history of human beings; we are not contributing curiosities however, but observations which no one has doubted, but which have escaped remark only because they are always before our eyes. 99
>
> Ludwig Wittgenstein, *Philosophical Investigations*

enough basis for an understanding of actual utterances. To truly comprehend what is being said, you need to know, too, the social context, as well as the speaker's purposes and intentions.

Philosophers interested in constructing theories of meaning for languages have had to account for the importance of context—a point repeatedly emphasized by Wittgenstein. One response to this issue dates back to the work of British language philosopher Paul Grice* in the 1950s and 1960s. This response is still popular today and involves distinguishing semantics* from pragmatics* and seeing them as two distinct and separate parts of linguistics.

Semantics examines what speakers know by virtue of knowing a language. However, this is not to understand what people say in everyday conversation. People can use the same expression to mean different things in different contexts. However, despite two possible meanings, we are usually able to grasp what they mean. Pragmatics studies the knowledge and skills that allow us to do this.

American philosopher David Kaplan,[1] for example, has distinguished between "character" and "content"—meaning the character of a sentence is constant, but its content alters in different circumstances. Similarly, contextualists* in linguistics have attempted to formulate theories to explain the absolute importance of context to understanding.

Schools Of Thought

From the 1960s on, a new generation of Wittgensteinian philosophers emerged. These thinkers, by and large, had not had significant personal contact with Wittgenstein, but had been inspired by reading his works, especially *Philosophical Investigations*. Many members of this group were based in the United States, rather than in Britain, and included Stanley Cavell* and Cora Diamond.*

There were many areas of traditional philosophy that Wittgenstein did not explicitly address in *Investigations*. One of the contributions of the Wittgensteinian philosophers mentioned above is that they extended his insights into topics that he himself had never, or rarely, mentioned. For example, *Investigations* and, in fact, the rest of Wittgenstein's work, include very little discussion of ethics*. Yet Diamond and others have approached ethics from a Wittgensteinian point of view, emphasizing how ethical concepts, like good or virtue, are used in ordinary human life and discourse.

Similarly, early readers of *Investigations* might have thought that traditional epistemology,* the theory of knowledge, was simply not possible in a Wittgensteinian context. Questions of language and meaning, they might assume, simply replace questions of how knowledge is possible. However, thinkers such as Thompson Clarke* and Stanley Cavell* showed that epistemological problems still arise. They also demonstrated how the ideas in *Investigations* shed light on epistemology.

In particular, these thinkers have used Wittgenstein's ideas to explore the old problem of skepticism.* The skeptic says that genuine, objective knowledge of the world is not possible. Traditionally, epistemologists have been concerned with this challenge to the possibility of knowledge and have set out to prove the skeptic wrong. Clarke, Cavell and others have explored what skepticism means and in what senses it can or cannot be proved or disproved.[2]

In Current Scholarship

Today, philosophers like Robert Brandom* and John McDowell* approach philosophical problems in a distinctively Wittgensteinian way—although they disagree on many important philosophical issues.

Wittgenstein himself criticized the construction of grand theories in philosophy and urged philosophers to adopt a piecemeal approach to their work. However, not all of his disciples have followed this advice. Robert Brandom, for instance, is engaged in the construction of a methodical theory of linguistic meaning, sometimes called "inferential role semantics."* Brandom sees Wittgenstein as an inspiration in this project. To simplify a little, Brandom regards the meaning of a linguistic expression as fixed by the *way* it is used, and he connects this with the Wittgensteinian slogan that "meaning is use."

Other followers have rejected this highly theoretical approach and prefer to continue in Wittgenstein's footsteps by looking to get rid of confusions, rather than constructing theories. One of the most influential people using this approach is the British philosopher John McDowell, especially since the publication in 1994 of his influential work, *Mind and World*.[3]

McDowell, like other Wittgensteinians, denies the possibility of what he calls a "sideways on" view of language and mind. We cannot do justice to the mind without using the correct terminology, he contends. We cannot, for example, describe mental phenomena in purely neuroscientific* terms, merely studying the nervous system and particularly the brain. If we do, we will miss some crucial aspects of mind. We cannot understand the mind without considering the ways we describe and make sense of each other in everyday life.

NOTES

1   David Kaplan, "Demonstratives," in *Themes from Kaplan,* ed. Joseph Almog et al (Oxford: Oxford University Press, 1989).

2   Thompson Clarke, "The Legacy of Skepticism," *Journal of Philosophy* 64 (1979): 754–69; Stanley Cavell, *The Claim of Reason* (Oxford: Oxford University Press, 1979).

3   John McDowell, *Mind and World* (Cambridge, Mass.: Harvard University Press, 1994).

IMPACT AND INFLUENCE TODAY

KEY POINTS

- Scholars and others still widely study *Philosophical Investigations,* and we can see its influence in the work of many contemporary philosophers. However, it is probably less influential than it was in the 1950s and 1960s.
- The book challenges representationalism—the idea that mental states function by representing the way the world is.
- Philosophers have responded, in part, by integrating their views on traditional philosophical issues with contemporary scientific knowledge.

Position

Within the philosophical community, people do not agree on the value and significance of *Philosophical Investigations.* But it is probably true to say that the book has less of an impact today than it did in the 1950s and 1960s. Metaphysics,* under the influence of philosophers such as Saul Kripke* and David Lewis,* has become the principal contemporary focus and goes against the spirit of *Investigations.* Metaphysics concentrates on theorizing about the nature of the world itself, rather than on how we understand it.

Overall, many present-day analytical philosophers, looking at connections between philosophy and science through language, do not think questions of language are as central to philosophy as Wittgenstein and his contemporaries did in the middle of the twentieth century. It remains to be seen, however, whether this is a temporary trend or a permanent state of affairs.

Early critics of the book concentrated on its lessons for the

> ** 66 ** We all stand, or should stand, in the shadow of
> Wittgenstein, in the same way that much earlier
> generations once stood in the shadow of Kant... **99**
> Michael Dummett*, *The Logical Basis of Metaphysics*

philosophy of mind. In particular, Wittgenstein's "private language
argument"* seemed to suggest that one could not speak meaningfully
of a person's private sensations. That led to the interpretation of
Wittgenstein as a sort of behaviorist*—that is, as saying that the
meaning of a sentence like, "Paul is in pain," is to be understood in
terms of Paul's external behavior rather than his inner sensations.

After the publication of Kripke's *Wittgenstein on Rules and Private
Language* in 1982,[1] the focus shifted greatly to Wittgenstein's views on
the philosophy of language. Critics have disputed Kripke's
interpretation of Wittgenstein, and most would probably question its
accuracy, but he did spark a new debate on how Wittgenstein's ideas
can be applied to contemporary discussions about meaning.

Interaction

Philosophical Investigations challenged the dominant view in the
philosophy of mind, sometimes called representationalism,* a view
also accepted in much of theoretical psychology and cognitive science,
the interdisciplinary study of the mind.* Representationalists believe
that mental states work by representing the world. They have truth
conditions: they state that the world is a certain way. Wittgenstein
implicitly questions this model of understanding the mind in
Investigations. He suggests representation turns out to be a very
particular notion, one that has a legitimate use, but is not applicable to
all mental states.

More broadly, Wittgenstein's work contrasts what science and
philosophy actually do. One of his themes is the idea that scientists

should be engaged in the task of constructing theories, but philosophers should not. The role of philosophy is to clear up confusions rather than add to our theoretical knowledge of the world. This challenges the way that philosophers have traditionally seen their discipline.

Critics inspired by Wittgenstein's writings have advanced these challenges to mainstream philosophy. It is a matter of controversy, however, as to how true such critics are to the intentions of Wittgenstein himself. The correct interpretation of his philosophy is still a matter of debate.

The Continuing Debate

Defenders of representationalism in the philosophy of mind have modified their views in order to take account of Wittgensteinian criticisms. Representationalists describe the mind as representing or reflecting the world, or as stating that the world is a certain way. Much recent debate has focused on the issue of perception. On this point, representationalists believe that seeing an apple on a table involves forming a mental picture (representation) of an apple on a table.

In the past, that view was often assumed rather than asserted and defended. Partly due to the pressure of Wittgensteinian criticisms, recent supporters of this view have begun to formulate arguments to back up their claim. They have also examined more closely the issue of precisely what perceptual representations are. The philosopher Susanna Siegel,* for example, has examined these issues with the intention of strengthening the defenses of representationalism against these criticisms.

While these responses to Wittgenstein's arguments do not necessarily come from a single philosophical perspective, it is possible to identify a common theme. Representationalism in philosophy of mind is essentially a naturalistic* movement. It happily connects the philosophy of mind with developments in cognitive science and empirical psychology.* This is a similar approach to that of the philosophy of language mentioned above—attempting to address issues of meaning in a scientific manner.

Collectively, then, these philosophers are trying to reintegrate philosophy and science, disciplines that Wittgenstein believed to be quite separate. They are advocates of a more scientific world view than Wittgenstein thought possible or desirable.

NOTES

1   Saul Kripke, *Wittgenstein on Rules and Private Language* (Oxford: Blackwell, 1982).

MODULE 12
WHERE NEXT?

KEY POINTS

- Contextualists* in philosophy of language and in epistemology (the philosophy of knowledge) continue to draw inspiration from Wittgenstein's ideas.

- *Philosophical Investigations* emphasizes the importance of the human in determining meaning.

- *Investigations* is a complex text with implications for many areas of philosophy. It will continue to be a source of inspiration and disagreement.

Potential

Ludwig Wittgenstein's *Philosophical Investigations* is probably less influential today than it was in the first 20 years after its publication. However, it is still very widely read and studied. Two recently popular philosophical views that have some affinities with Wittgenstein's arguments may affect its future influence. Both these views are frequently known as "contextualism:"* one in the philosophy of language and the other in epistemology,* the theory of knowledge.

In the philosophy of language, contextualism is the view that the meaning of what someone says is profoundly affected by its context. When I say a sentence in English, its meaning is not determined by facts about English. To discover what it means, we must look at the situation in which I spoke. Arguably, this is a view that Wittgenstein puts forward in *Philosophical Investigations*. Certainly, the contemporary supporters of this argument draw inspiration from Wittgenstein's views.

> ❝ For Wittgenstein, philosophy comes to grief not in denying what we all know to be true, but in its effort to escape those human forms of life which alone provide the coherence of our expression. He wishes an acknowledgement of human limitation which does not leave us chafed by our own skin, by a sense of powerlessness to penetrate beyond the human conditions of knowledge. ❞
>
> Stanley Cavell, *The Availability of Wittgenstein's Later Philosophy*

In epistemology, contextualism is the view that what counts as knowledge in one context may not count as knowledge in another. I may believe I know, for everyday purposes, that a colleague is trustworthy. But if I am a witness in a court of law, where higher standards of evidence are demanded, I may not count on knowing this. Wittgenstein put forward something like this view in his late work *On Certainty*, but it also has roots in *Investigations*.

Future Directions

Some influential contemporary thinkers, such as the American philosopher Charles Travis,* have drawn inspiration from Wittgenstein in arguing for forms of contextualism in the philosophy of language. Travis calls for a very radical form of contextualism. In his books *The Uses of Sense*[1] and *Thought's Footing*,[2] he draws on *Investigations* and Wittgenstein's other late writings to support his argument that the context in which language is used has a very deep and extensive role in determining meaning.

Another American philosopher, Michael Williams,* has used Wittgenstein's writings to argue for contextualism in epistemology, especially in his book *Unnatural Doubts*.[3] Williams claims that certain concepts in Wittgenstein's work undermine skepticism:* the view that genuine knowledge of the world is impossible. Skeptics have argued, for example, that I cannot truly know that there is a cup on my desk because it is possible that I am merely dreaming or hallucinating the presence of a cup.

Williams argues that skeptical doubts do not always need to be taken seriously. Doubts arise in particular contexts: when, for example, I have particular reason to suppose that things are not as they seem. Wittgenstein's lesson here, as always, is that meaning depends on context. Doubts may make sense in one context, but not in another.

Summary

Wittgenstein's *Philosophical Investigations* was a crucially important text in the development of analyitical philosophy★ in the twentieth century. It revolutionized the philosophy of language by paying previously unheard of attention to ordinary langauge. It revealed the true complexity of such langue and so began a move awat from the formal models of language that philosophers had used in the past.

his work also drew attention to the diversity and complexity of debates about the human mind providing a fresh impetus for the philosophy of mind, which has been in the centre of philosophical reasearch ever since. It raised crucial questions, too, about the nature and everyday workings of philosophy itself: how much can philosophy achieve and how much should it attempt to achieve?

This is a very rich book. It continues to be a source of new ideas and inspiration for philosophers and students, and its ideas have by no means been exhausted. And while its unusual style makes it difficult to master (a long series of related remarks rather than a continuous argument), it has proven very important in inspiring new and original work by philosophers.

To summarize the significance of the work, you might say that it marked a return to an emphasis on the role of the human. Notions crucial to philosophy like truth, meaning, and representation are not abstractions remote from human experience, Wittgenstein said, but can be understood by examining the human contexts in which they are actually used.

Wittgenstein can be regarded as a kind of naturalist,* even though he is often seen as anti-naturalist. Why? Because he opposed the view that the natural sciences can ultimately solve all intellectual problems, including philosophical ones. But he is a naturalist in a broader sense, believing that the ideas that create philosophical problems do not transcend human experience, but are part of it and find their meaning in their use in life.

Perhaps, then, the future importance of *Philosophical Investigations* will lie in acknowledgement of the human origins of all the words and concepts that affect abstract philosophical problems.

NOTES

1   Charles Travis, *The Uses of Sense: Wittgenstein's Philosophy of Language* (Oxford: Clarendon, 1989).

2   Charles Travis, *Thought's Footing* (Oxford: Clarendon, 2006).

3   Michael Williams, *Unnatural Doubts: Epistemological Realism and the Basis of Scepticism* (Oxford: Blackwell, 1991).

GLOSSARY

GLOSSARY OF TERMS

Analytical philosophy: an influential twentieth-century philosophical movement—associated particularly with Britain, Germany, and the United States—that emphasized logic, language, and the connections between philosophy and science.

Anthropology: the scientific study of human beings and culture.

Aspect perception: the phenomenon whereby the same object can be perceived in different ways. A drawing, for example, may be perceived either as a picture of a duck or a picture of a rabbit.

Behaviorism: the view that mental states should be understood in terms of behavior—for example, that being angry is essentially a matter of behaving in an angry fashion.

Cognitive science: the interdisciplinary study of the mind, encompassing parts of psychology, philosophy, linguistics, and computer science.

Conceptual analysis: a philosophical method using the analysis of words and concepts to discover their meanings.

Contextualism: the view that the meaning of a word or sentence is dependent on the context in which the word or sentence is used.

Empiricism: the view that all human knowledge comes from experience.

Epistemology: a branch of philosophy dealing with knowledge.

Ethics: a branch of philosophy dealing with morality and what is good.

Fideism: the view that religious belief is based in faith rather than reason.

Gestalt school: a school of psychologists prominent in Germany and Austria in the early twentieth century that advocated that perception should be understood in an integrated manner. Its leading figure was perhaps Wolfgang Köhler (1887–1967).

Inferential role semantics: the view that the meaning of an expression should be understood in terms of its inferential roles with other expressions, rather than its truth conditions.

Intentionality: the object-directedness or "aboutness" of a state. Fear is intentional, for example, insofar as it is fear *of* something.

Language games: a simple scenario in which speakers use words or sentences for particular purposes and according to definite rules.

Logic: a branch of mathematics and philosophy dealing with reasoning in general and inference in particular.

Logical atomism: the philosophical view that all meaningful sentences are constructed logically from basic or atomic sentences about simple objects or logical atoms.

Logical positivism: a radical philosophical movement—active from the late 1920s, especially in Austria and Germany—that emphasizes the logical analysis of language.

Mental entity: something that exists in the mind, arguably including ideas, thoughts, feelings and experiences.

Metaphysics: a branch of philosophy dealing with the ultimate or fundamental constituents of reality, with what there fundamentally is.

Modernism: a movement in literature, music, art, and architecture, particularly in the early twentieth century, characterized by a decisive break with tradition.

Naturalism: in philosophy, the view that philosophy and science are engaged in the same project and use essentially the same methods.

Neuroscience: the scientific study of the nervous system, including the brain.

Ordinary language philosophy: a school of philosophy associated particularly with the University of Oxford in the 1950s and 1960s, emphasizing careful attention to language use.

Philosophy as therapy: philosophical writing aimed at removing intellectual problems and confusions rather than arriving at new truths about the world.

Pragmatics: the study of the rules and conventions that govern the use of language.

Private experience: an experience that cannot be adequately described in language and can therefore only be understood by the person who has the experience.

Private language: a language that can be understood only by one person.

Representationalism: the view that language and mind function primarily by representing the world accurately or inaccurately.

Skepticism: the view that genuine knowledge of the world is impossible.

Scientism: the view that all-important intellectual questions can be answered by the methods of science.

Semantics: the study of linguistic meaning.

Sense data: mental entities that some philosophers think are the direct objects of perceptual experience. It is sometimes believed, for example, that the direct objects of vision are color patches, or that the direct objects of hearing are sounds.

Sociology: the scientific study of society.

Theology: the study of the nature of God and God's attributes.

World War I (1914–1918): a major conflict involving all of the main European powers (primarily Germany, France, and Great Britain) and a number of other world powers, including the United States and Japan.

PEOPLE MENTIONED IN THE TEXT

Elizabeth Anscombe (1919–2001) was a British philosopher. A student of Wittgenstein's, she became perhaps the leading Wittgensteinian philosopher of the post-war period.

John L. Austin (1911–60) was a British philosopher and a leader of the so-called "ordinary language" school of philosophy. He made major contributions to both the philosophy of language and the philosophy of perception.

Alain Badiou (b. 1937) is a French philosopher. He has written on metaphysics and set theory.

Ludwig van Beethoven (1770–1827) was a German composer. His symphonic and chamber works are frequently regarded as forming a bridge between the classical and romantic musical eras.

David Bloor (b. 1942) is a British sociologist. He is best known as a founder of the "Edinburgh school," which seeks to understand science in sociological terms.

Jacques Bouveresse (b. 1940) is a French philosopher. He has defended and developed analytical philosophy in a style more usually associated with the English-speaking world.

Robert Brandom (b. 1950) is an American philosopher. He has written widely on the philosophy of language and mind, as well as the history of philosophy.

Rudolph Carnap (1891–1970) was a German philosopher and

leader of the logical positivist movement. He contributed to logic, the philosophy of language and the philosophy of science.

Stanley Cavell (b. 1926) is an American philosopher. He has written widely on Wittgenstein, philosophy, and the arts, particularly cinema.

Thompson Clarke (1928–2012) was an American philosopher. Although he published only two short articles, Clarke was influential in epistemology.

Nicolaus Copernicus (1473–1543) was a Polish astronomer and mathematician. He advocated heliocentrism, according to which the sun and not the earth is at the center of the solar system.

Donald Davidson (1917–2003) was an American philosopher of language. His writings on philosophy of language and philosophy of mind became highly influential from the 1970s.

Cora Diamond (b. 1937) is an American philosopher. She has written widely on ethics, philosophy of language, and Wittgenstein.

Michael Dummett (1925–2011) was a British philosopher. He was both an influential philosopher of language in his own right and the leading interpreter of the works of Frege.

Gottlob Frege (1848–1925) was a German mathematician and philosopher. Though little known during his lifetime, his work in logic and the philosophy of language later revolutionized those subjects.

Sigmund Freud (1856–1939) was a German psychologist and the founder of psychoanalysis. He suggested that a system of unconscious drives and repressions determines much of human behavior.

Peter Geach (1916–2013) was a British philosopher. He wrote widely on logic, language, and the history of philosophy.

H. P. Grice (1913–88) was a British philosopher of language. He is considered an important figure in both philosophy and linguistics and a founder of the discipline of pragmatics.

Peter Hacker (b. 1939) is a British philosopher. He is one of the foremost interpreters of Wittgenstein's work.

Martin Heidegger (1889–1976) was a German philosopher. He is associated with the phenomenological school, which flourished in Germany and France in the early twentieth century and aimed to study consciousness from the subjective, first person point of view.

Derek Jarman (1942–94) was an English filmmaker. He is known for his experimental film style and for tackling controversial topics.

Immanuel Kant (1724–1804) was a German philosopher. He was the author of *The Critique of Pure Reason* (1781) and perhaps the most influential philosopher of the modern era.

David Kaplan (b. 1933) is an American philosopher. He has contributed important ideas to the philosophy of language.

Gustav Klimt (1862–1918) was an Austrian painter. His work is marked by an unconventional style and frank eroticism.

Saul Kripke (b. 1940) is an American philosopher. He has contributed to logic, philosophy of language, and numerous other fields, and he is widely regarded as one of the most important contemporary philosophers.

Thomas Kuhn (1922–96) was an American philosopher and historian of science. He is best known for emphasizing the importance of historical conditions in the formation of scientific knowledge.

John McDowell (b. 1942) is a British philosopher. He has written on many topics, including Aristotle, ethics, epistemology, and the philosophy of mind.

Norman Malcolm (1911–90) was an American philosopher. He contributed to epistemology and was one of the first generation of Wittgenstein scholars in the United States.

Wolfgang Amadeus Mozart (1756–91) was an Austrian composer. His symphonies, masses, operas, and concertos are considered central works of the classical era of music.

Kai Nielsen (b. 1926) is a Canadian philosopher. He has written widely on the philosophy of religion.

D. Z. Phillips (1934–2006) was a Welsh philosopher. Profoundly influenced by Wittgenstein, he wrote widely on ethics, literature, and religion.

Karl Popper (1902–94) was an Austrian philosopher. He is one of the best-known philosophers of science of the twentieth century.

Frank Ramsey (1903–30) was an English philosopher, economist, and mathematician. He was one of the first commentators on Wittgenstein's works and assisted in the first English translation of the *Tractatus Logico-Philosophicus*.

Rush Rhees (1905–89) was a British philosopher. He applied Wittgensteinian ideas to the philosophy of religion.

I. A. Richards (1893–1979) was an English literary critic. He wrote poetry as well as influential works of literary theory.

Richard Rorty (1931–2007) was an American philosopher. He was a radical critic of contemporary philosophical trends and wrote widely on literature as well as the philosophy of language.

Bertrand Russell (1872–1970) was a British philosopher, logician, social commentator, and political activist. His early work on logic and the basics of mathematics helped to lay the foundations of analytical philosophy.

Gilbert Ryle (1900–76) was a leading British philosopher. Often associated with the so-called "ordinary language" school, his most important contributions were to the philosophy of mind.

Arnold Schoenberg (1874–1951) was an Austrian composer. His music was revolutionary, particularly because of his break with traditional harmony.

Franz Schubert (1797–1828) was an Austrian composer. His many symphonic and chamber works and songs are regarded as major examples of early romantic music.

John Searle (b. 1932) is an American philosopher. He has contributed both to the philosophy of language and the philosophy of mind.

Susanna Siegel is an American philosopher who is currently the

Edgar Pierce Professor of Philosophy at Harvard University. Her main focus is on epistemology and the philosophy of mind.

Charles Travis (b. 1943) is an American philosopher. He is a noted advocate of radical contextualism in the philosophy of language.

David Foster Wallace (1962–2008) was an American writer. He is known for his novels and also his nonfiction work.

Alfred North Whitehead (1861–1947) was a British mathematician and philosopher. He is known both for his foundational work in mathematical logic and his work in metaphysics.

Michael Williams (b. 1947) is an American philosopher. He has written widely on epistemology and on Wittgenstein.

Georg Henrik von Wright (1916–2003) was a Finnish philosopher. He wrote widely on logic and the philosophy of language.

WORKS CITED

WORKS CITED

Anscombe, Elizabeth. *Intention*. Oxford: Blackwell, 1958.

——. "Modern Moral Philosophy," *Philosophy* 33, no. 124 (1958): 435–55.

Badiou, Alain. *Being and Event*. London: Continuum, 2005.

Bloor, David. *Wittgenstein, Rules and Institutions*. London: Routledge, 1997.

Braver, Lee. *Groundless Grounds: a Study of Wittgenstein and Heidegger*. Cambridge, Mass.: MIT Press, 2012.

Cavell, Stanley. *The Claim of Reason*. Oxford: Oxford University Press, 1979.

Clarke, Thompson. "The Legacy of Skepticism," *Journal of Philosophy* 64 (1972), pp. 754–69.

Dummett, Michael. *Truth and Other Enigmas*. London: Duckworth, 1978.

Frege, Gottlob. *Foundations of Arithmetic*. Translated by J. L. Austin. Oxford: Blackwell, 1950.

Geach, Peter. *Mental Acts: their Content and their Objects*. London: Routledge, 1957.

Guetti, James. *Wittgenstein and the Grammar of Literary Experience*. Athens GA: University of Georgia Press, 1993.

Hacker, Peter. *Insight and Illusion*. Oxford: Clarendon Press, 1972.

——. *Wittgenstein: Connections and Controversies*. Oxford: Oxford University Press, 2013.

Horwich, Paul. *Wittgenstein's Metaphilosophy*. Oxford: Oxford University Press, 2013.

Kaplan, David. "Demonstratives," *Themes from Kaplan*. Edited by Joseph Almog, John Perry and Howard Wettstein. Oxford: Oxford University Press, 1989.

Kerr, Fergus. *Theology after Wittgenstein*. Oxford: Blackwell, 1986.

Kripke, Saul. *Naming and Necessity*. Oxford: Blackwell, 1980.

——. *Wittgenstein on Rules and Private Language*. Oxford: Blackwell, 1982.

Kuhn, Thomas. *The Structure of Scientific Revolutions*. Chicago: University of Chicago Press, 1962.

Malcolm, Norman. *Dreaming*. London: Routledge and Kegan Paul, 1959.

Monk, Ray. *Ludwig Wittgenstein: the Duty of Genius*. London: Vintage, 1991.

Moyal-Sharrock, Daniel, ed. *The Third Wittgenstein*. Aldershot: Ashgate, 2004.

McDowell, John. *Mind and World*. Cambridge, Mass.: Harvard University Press, 1994.

Neilsen, Kai and D.Z. Phillips. *Wittgensteinian Fideism?* London: SCM Press, 2005.

Pears, David. *Wittgenstein*. London: Fontana, 1971.

——. *The False Prison*. Oxford: Clarendon Press, 1988.

Popper, Karl. *Conjectures and Refutations: the Growth of Scientific Knowledge*. London: Routledge, 2002.

Read, Rupert and Crary, Alice. *The New Wittgenstein*. London: Routledge, 2000.

Rorty, Richard. *Philosophy and the Mirror of Nature*. Princeton: Princeton University Press, 1979.

Russell, Bertrand. *The Principles of Mathematics*. London: Allen and Unwin, 1903.

——. *The Philosophy of Logical Atomism*. London: Routledge, 2009.

——. "On Denoting," *Mind* 14 (1905): 479–93.

——. *My Philosophical Development*. London: Allen and Unwin, 1959.

Russell, Bertrand, and Alfred North Whitehead. *Principia Mathematica.*

Cambridge: Cambridge University Press, 1910–13.

Searle, John. "Proper names," *Mind* 67 (1958): 166–73.

Travis, Charles. *Thought's Footing*. Oxford: Oxford University Press, 2006.

——. *The Uses of Sense: Wittgenstein's Philosophy of Language*. Oxford: Clarendon, 1989.

Williams, Michael. *Unnatural Doubts: Epistemological Realism and the Basis of Scepticism*. Oxford: Blackwell, 1991.

Williamson, Timothy. *The Philosophy of Philosophy*. Oxford: Blackwell, 2007.

Wittgenstein, Ludwig. *Philosophical Investigations*. Translated by Elizabeth Anscombe. Oxford: Blackwell, 2001.

——. *The Blue and Brown Books*. Oxford: Blackwell, 1958.

——. *On Certainty*. Translated by Denis Paul and G. E. M. Anscombe. Oxford: Blackwell, 1969.

——. *Philosophical Grammar*. Edited by Rush Rhees. Translated by Anthony Kenny. Oxford: Blackwell, 1974.

——. *Philosophical Remarks*. Edited by Rush Rhees. Translated by Raymond Hargreaves and Roger White. Oxford: Blackwell, 1975.

——. *Remarks on the Philosophy of Psychology*. Vol. 1. Edited by G. E. M. Anscombe and G. H. von Wright. Translated by G. E. M. Anscombe. Oxford: Blackwell, 1980.

——. *Remarks on the Philosophy of Psychology*. Vol. 2. Edited by G. H. von Wright and Heikki Nyman. Translated by C. G. Luckhardt and M. A. E. Aue. Oxford: Blackwell, 1980.

——. *Philosophical Investigations*. Translated by Elizabeth Anscombe. Oxford: Blackwell, 2001.

——. *Tractatus Logico-Philosophicus*. Translated by David Pears and Brian McGuinness. London: Routledge and Kegan Paul, 1974.

——. *Lectures and Conversations on Aesthetics, Philosophy and Religious Belief*. Edited by Cyril Barrett. Oxford: Blackwell, 1967.

——. *Wittgenstein in Cambridge: Letters and Documents 1911–1951*. Edited by Brian McGuinness. Malden MA: Blackwell, 2008.

——. "Some Remarks on Logical Form," *Proceedings of the Aristotelian Society*, Supplementary Volume 9 (1929), 162–71.

THE MACAT LIBRARY
BY DISCIPLINE

AFRICANA STUDIES

Chinua Achebe's *An Image of Africa: Racism in Conrad's Heart of Darkness*
W. E. B. Du Bois's *The Souls of Black Folk*
Zora Neale Huston's *Characteristics of Negro Expression*
Martin Luther King Jr's *Why We Can't Wait*
Toni Morrison's *Playing in the Dark: Whiteness in the American Literary Imagination*

ANTHROPOLOGY

Arjun Appadurai's *Modernity at Large: Cultural Dimensions of Globalisation*
Philippe Ariès's *Centuries of Childhood*
Franz Boas's *Race, Language and Culture*
Kim Chan & Renée Mauborgne's *Blue Ocean Strategy*
Jared Diamond's *Guns, Germs & Steel: the Fate of Human Societies*
Jared Diamond's *Collapse: How Societies Choose to Fail or Survive*
E. E. Evans-Pritchard's *Witchcraft, Oracles and Magic Among the Azande*
James Ferguson's *The Anti-Politics Machine*
Clifford Geertz's *The Interpretation of Cultures*
David Graeber's *Debt: the First 5000 Years*
Karen Ho's *Liquidated: An Ethnography of Wall Street*
Geert Hofstede's *Culture's Consequences: Comparing Values, Behaviors, Institutes and Organizations across Nations*
Claude Lévi-Strauss's *Structural Anthropology*
Jay Macleod's *Ain't No Makin' It: Aspirations and Attainment in a Low-Income Neighborhood*
Saba Mahmood's *The Politics of Piety: The Islamic Revival and the Feminist Subject*
Marcel Mauss's *The Gift*

BUSINESS

Jean Lave & Etienne Wenger's *Situated Learning*
Theodore Levitt's *Marketing Myopia*
Burton G. Malkiel's *A Random Walk Down Wall Street*
Douglas McGregor's *The Human Side of Enterprise*
Michael Porter's *Competitive Strategy: Creating and Sustaining Superior Performance*
John Kotter's *Leading Change*
C. K. Prahalad & Gary Hamel's *The Core Competence of the Corporation*

CRIMINOLOGY

Michelle Alexander's *The New Jim Crow: Mass Incarceration in the Age of Colorblindness*
Michael R. Gottfredson & Travis Hirschi's *A General Theory of Crime*
Richard Herrnstein & Charles A. Murray's *The Bell Curve: Intelligence and Class Structure in American Life*
Elizabeth Loftus's *Eyewitness Testimony*
Jay Macleod's *Ain't No Makin' It: Aspirations and Attainment in a Low-Income Neighborhood*
Philip Zimbardo's *The Lucifer Effect*

ECONOMICS

Janet Abu Lughod's *Before European Hegemony*
Ha-Joon Chang's *Kicking Away the Ladder*
David Brion Davis's *The Problem of Slavery in the Age of Revolution*
Milton Friedman's *The Role of Monetary Policy*
Milton Friedman's *Capitalism and Freedom*
David Graeber's *Debt: the First 5000 Years*
Friedrich Hayek's *The Road to Serfdom*
Karen Ho's *Liquidated: An Ethnography of Wall Street*

The Macat Library By Discipline

John Maynard Keynes's *The General Theory of Employment, Interest and Money*
Charles P. Kindleberger's *Manias, Panics and Crashes*
Robert Lucas's *Why Doesn't Capital Flow from Rich to Poor Countries?*
Burton G. Malkiel's *A Random Walk Down Wall Street*
Thomas Robert Malthus's *An Essay on the Principle of Population*
Karl Marx's *Capital*
Thomas Piketty's *Capital in the Twenty-First Century*
Amartya Sen's *Development as Freedom*
Adam Smith's *The Wealth of Nations*
Nassim Nicholas Taleb's *The Black Swan: The Impact of the Highly Improbable*
Amos Tversky's & Daniel Kahneman's *Judgment under Uncertainty: Heuristics and Biases*
Mahbub Ul Haq's *Reflections on Human Development*
Max Weber's *The Protestant Ethic and the Spirit of Capitalism*

FEMINISM AND GENDER STUDIES

Judith Butler's *Gender Trouble*
Simone De Beauvoir's *The Second Sex*
Michel Foucault's *History of Sexuality*
Betty Friedan's *The Feminine Mystique*
Saba Mahmood's *The Politics of Piety: The Islamic Revival and the Feminist Subject*
Joan Wallach Scott's *Gender and the Politics of History*
Mary Wollstonecraft's *A Vindication of the Rights of Woman*
Virginia Woolf's *A Room of One's Own*

GEOGRAPHY

The Brundtland Report's *Our Common Future*
Rachel Carson's *Silent Spring*
Charles Darwin's *On the Origin of Species*
James Ferguson's *The Anti-Politics Machine*
Jane Jacobs's *The Death and Life of Great American Cities*
James Lovelock's *Gaia: A New Look at Life on Earth*
Amartya Sen's *Development as Freedom*
Mathis Wackernagel & William Rees's *Our Ecological Footprint*

HISTORY

Janet Abu-Lughod's *Before European Hegemony*
Benedict Anderson's *Imagined Communities*
Bernard Bailyn's *The Ideological Origins of the American Revolution*
Hanna Batatu's *The Old Social Classes And The Revolutionary Movements Of Iraq*
Christopher Browning's *Ordinary Men: Reserve Police Batallion 101 and the Final Solution in Poland*
Edmund Burke's *Reflections on the Revolution in France*
William Cronon's *Nature's Metropolis: Chicago And The Great West*
Alfred W. Crosby's *The Columbian Exchange*
Hamid Dabashi's *Iran: A People Interrupted*
David Brion Davis's *The Problem of Slavery in the Age of Revolution*
Nathalie Zemon Davis's *The Return of Martin Guerre*
Jared Diamond's *Guns, Germs & Steel: the Fate of Human Societies*
Frank Dikotter's *Mao's Great Famine*
John W Dower's *War Without Mercy: Race And Power In The Pacific War*
W. E. B. Du Bois's *The Souls of Black Folk*
Richard J. Evans's *In Defence of History*
Lucien Febvre's *The Problem of Unbelief in the 16th Century*
Sheila Fitzpatrick's *Everyday Stalinism*

Eric Foner's *Reconstruction: America's Unfinished Revolution, 1863-1877*
Michel Foucault's *Discipline and Punish*
Michel Foucault's *History of Sexuality*
Francis Fukuyama's *The End of History and the Last Man*
John Lewis Gaddis's *We Now Know: Rethinking Cold War History*
Ernest Gellner's *Nations and Nationalism*
Eugene Genovese's *Roll, Jordan, Roll: The World the Slaves Made*
Carlo Ginzburg's *The Night Battles*
Daniel Goldhagen's *Hitler's Willing Executioners*
Jack Goldstone's *Revolution and Rebellion in the Early Modern World*
Antonio Gramsci's *The Prison Notebooks*
Alexander Hamilton, John Jay & James Madison's *The Federalist Papers*
Christopher Hill's *The World Turned Upside Down*
Carole Hillenbrand's *The Crusades: Islamic Perspectives*
Thomas Hobbes's *Leviathan*
Eric Hobsbawm's *The Age Of Revolution*
John A. Hobson's *Imperialism: A Study*
Albert Hourani's *History of the Arab Peoples*
Samuel P. Huntington's *The Clash of Civilizations and the Remaking of World Order*
C. L. R. James's *The Black Jacobins*
Tony Judt's *Postwar: A History of Europe Since 1945*
Ernst Kantorowicz's *The King's Two Bodies: A Study in Medieval Political Theology*
Paul Kennedy's *The Rise and Fall of the Great Powers*
Ian Kershaw's *The "Hitler Myth": Image and Reality in the Third Reich*
John Maynard Keynes's *The General Theory of Employment, Interest and Money*
Charles P. Kindleberger's *Manias, Panics and Crashes*
Martin Luther King Jr's *Why We Can't Wait*
Henry Kissinger's *World Order: Reflections on the Character of Nations and the Course of History*
Thomas Kuhn's *The Structure of Scientific Revolutions*
Georges Lefebvre's *The Coming of the French Revolution*
John Locke's *Two Treatises of Government*
Niccolò Machiavelli's *The Prince*
Thomas Robert Malthus's *An Essay on the Principle of Population*
Mahmood Mamdani's *Citizen and Subject: Contemporary Africa And The Legacy Of Late Colonialism*
Karl Marx's *Capital*
Stanley Milgram's *Obedience to Authority*
John Stuart Mill's *On Liberty*
Thomas Paine's *Common Sense*
Thomas Paine's *Rights of Man*
Geoffrey Parker's *Global Crisis: War, Climate Change and Catastrophe in the Seventeenth Century*
Jonathan Riley-Smith's *The First Crusade and the Idea of Crusading*
Jean-Jacques Rousseau's *The Social Contract*
Joan Wallach Scott's *Gender and the Politics of History*
Theda Skocpol's *States and Social Revolutions*
Adam Smith's *The Wealth of Nations*
Timothy Snyder's *Bloodlands: Europe Between Hitler and Stalin*
Sun Tzu's *The Art of War*
Keith Thomas's *Religion and the Decline of Magic*
Thucydides's *The History of the Peloponnesian War*
Frederick Jackson Turner's *The Significance of the Frontier in American History*
Odd Arne Westad's *The Global Cold War: Third World Interventions And The Making Of Our Times*

The Macat Library By Discipline

LITERATURE

Chinua Achebe's *An Image of Africa: Racism in Conrad's Heart of Darkness*
Roland Barthes's *Mythologies*
Homi K. Bhabha's *The Location of Culture*
Judith Butler's *Gender Trouble*
Simone De Beauvoir's *The Second Sex*
Ferdinand De Saussure's *Course in General Linguistics*
T. S. Eliot's *The Sacred Wood: Essays on Poetry and Criticism*
Zora Neale Huston's *Characteristics of Negro Expression*
Toni Morrison's *Playing in the Dark: Whiteness in the American Literary Imagination*
Edward Said's *Orientalism*
Gayatri Chakravorty Spivak's *Can the Subaltern Speak?*
Mary Wollstonecraft's *A Vindication of the Rights of Women*
Virginia Woolf's *A Room of One's Own*

PHILOSOPHY

Elizabeth Anscombe's *Modern Moral Philosophy*
Hannah Arendt's *The Human Condition*
Aristotle's *Metaphysics*
Aristotle's *Nicomachean Ethics*
Edmund Gettier's *Is Justified True Belief Knowledge?*
Georg Wilhelm Friedrich Hegel's *Phenomenology of Spirit*
David Hume's *Dialogues Concerning Natural Religion*
David Hume's *The Enquiry for Human Understanding*
Immanuel Kant's *Religion within the Boundaries of Mere Reason*
Immanuel Kant's *Critique of Pure Reason*
Søren Kierkegaard's *The Sickness Unto Death*
Søren Kierkegaard's *Fear and Trembling*
C. S. Lewis's *The Abolition of Man*
Alasdair MacIntyre's *After Virtue*
Marcus Aurelius's *Meditations*
Friedrich Nietzsche's *On the Genealogy of Morality*
Friedrich Nietzsche's *Beyond Good and Evil*
Plato's *Republic*
Plato's *Symposium*
Jean-Jacques Rousseau's *The Social Contract*
Gilbert Ryle's *The Concept of Mind*
Baruch Spinoza's *Ethics*
Sun Tzu's *The Art of War*
Ludwig Wittgenstein's *Philosophical Investigations*

POLITICS

Benedict Anderson's *Imagined Communities*
Aristotle's *Politics*
Bernard Bailyn's *The Ideological Origins of the American Revolution*
Edmund Burke's *Reflections on the Revolution in France*
John C. Calhoun's *A Disquisition on Government*
Ha-Joon Chang's *Kicking Away the Ladder*
Hamid Dabashi's *Iran: A People Interrupted*
Hamid Dabashi's *Theology of Discontent: The Ideological Foundation of the Islamic Revolution in Iran*
Robert Dahl's *Democracy and its Critics*
Robert Dahl's *Who Governs?*
David Brion Davis's *The Problem of Slavery in the Age of Revolution*

Alexis De Tocqueville's *Democracy in America*
James Ferguson's *The Anti-Politics Machine*
Frank Dikotter's *Mao's Great Famine*
Sheila Fitzpatrick's *Everyday Stalinism*
Eric Foner's *Reconstruction: America's Unfinished Revolution, 1863-1877*
Milton Friedman's *Capitalism and Freedom*
Francis Fukuyama's *The End of History and the Last Man*
John Lewis Gaddis's *We Now Know: Rethinking Cold War History*
Ernest Gellner's *Nations and Nationalism*
David Graeber's *Debt: the First 5000 Years*
Antonio Gramsci's *The Prison Notebooks*
Alexander Hamilton, John Jay & James Madison's *The Federalist Papers*
Friedrich Hayek's *The Road to Serfdom*
Christopher Hill's *The World Turned Upside Down*
Thomas Hobbes's *Leviathan*
John A. Hobson's *Imperialism: A Study*
Samuel P. Huntington's *The Clash of Civilizations and the Remaking of World Order*
Tony Judt's *Postwar: A History of Europe Since 1945*
David C. Kang's *China Rising: Peace, Power and Order in East Asia*
Paul Kennedy's *The Rise and Fall of Great Powers*
Robert Keohane's *After Hegemony*
Martin Luther King Jr.'s *Why We Can't Wait*
Henry Kissinger's *World Order: Reflections on the Character of Nations and the Course of History*
John Locke's *Two Treatises of Government*
Niccolò Machiavelli's *The Prince*
Thomas Robert Malthus's *An Essay on the Principle of Population*
Mahmood Mamdani's *Citizen and Subject: Contemporary Africa And The Legacy Of Late Colonialism*
Karl Marx's *Capital*
John Stuart Mill's *On Liberty*
John Stuart Mill's *Utilitarianism*
Hans Morgenthau's *Politics Among Nations*
Thomas Paine's *Common Sense*
Thomas Paine's *Rights of Man*
Thomas Piketty's *Capital in the Twenty-First Century*
Robert D. Putman's *Bowling Alone*
John Rawls's *Theory of Justice*
Jean-Jacques Rousseau's *The Social Contract*
Theda Skocpol's *States and Social Revolutions*
Adam Smith's *The Wealth of Nations*
Sun Tzu's *The Art of War*
Henry David Thoreau's *Civil Disobedience*
Thucydides's *The History of the Peloponnesian War*
Kenneth Waltz's *Theory of International Politics*
Max Weber's *Politics as a Vocation*
Odd Arne Westad's *The Global Cold War: Third World Interventions And The Making Of Our Times*

POSTCOLONIAL STUDIES

Roland Barthes's *Mythologies*
Frantz Fanon's *Black Skin, White Masks*
Homi K. Bhabha's *The Location of Culture*
Gustavo Gutiérrez's *A Theology of Liberation*
Edward Said's *Orientalism*
Gayatri Chakravorty Spivak's *Can the Subaltern Speak?*

The Macat Library By Discipline

PSYCHOLOGY

Gordon Allport's *The Nature of Prejudice*
Alan Baddeley & Graham Hitch's *Aggression: A Social Learning Analysis*
Albert Bandura's *Aggression: A Social Learning Analysis*
Leon Festinger's *A Theory of Cognitive Dissonance*
Sigmund Freud's *The Interpretation of Dreams*
Betty Friedan's *The Feminine Mystique*
Michael R. Gottfredson & Travis Hirschi's *A General Theory of Crime*
Eric Hoffer's *The True Believer: Thoughts on the Nature of Mass Movements*
William James's *Principles of Psychology*
Elizabeth Loftus's *Eyewitness Testimony*
A. H. Maslow's *A Theory of Human Motivation*
Stanley Milgram's *Obedience to Authority*
Steven Pinker's *The Better Angels of Our Nature*
Oliver Sacks's *The Man Who Mistook His Wife For a Hat*
Richard Thaler & Cass Sunstein's *Nudge: Improving Decisions About Health, Wealth and Happiness*
Amos Tversky's *Judgment under Uncertainty: Heuristics and Biases*
Philip Zimbardo's *The Lucifer Effect*

SCIENCE

Rachel Carson's *Silent Spring*
William Cronon's *Nature's Metropolis: Chicago And The Great West*
Alfred W. Crosby's *The Columbian Exchange*
Charles Darwin's *On the Origin of Species*
Richard Dawkin's *The Selfish Gene*
Thomas Kuhn's *The Structure of Scientific Revolutions*
Geoffrey Parker's *Global Crisis: War, Climate Change and Catastrophe in the Seventeenth Century*
Mathis Wackernagel & William Rees's *Our Ecological Footprint*

SOCIOLOGY

Michelle Alexander's *The New Jim Crow: Mass Incarceration in the Age of Colorblindness*
Gordon Allport's *The Nature of Prejudice*
Albert Bandura's *Aggression: A Social Learning Analysis*
Hanna Batatu's *The Old Social Classes And The Revolutionary Movements Of Iraq*
Ha-Joon Chang's *Kicking Away the Ladder*
W. E. B. Du Bois's *The Souls of Black Folk*
Émile Durkheim's *On Suicide*
Frantz Fanon's *Black Skin, White Masks*
Frantz Fanon's *The Wretched of the Earth*
Eric Foner's *Reconstruction: America's Unfinished Revolution, 1863-1877*
Eugene Genovese's *Roll, Jordan, Roll: The World the Slaves Made*
Jack Goldstone's *Revolution and Rebellion in the Early Modern World*
Antonio Gramsci's *The Prison Notebooks*
Richard Herrnstein & Charles A Murray's *The Bell Curve: Intelligence and Class Structure in American Life*
Eric Hoffer's *The True Believer: Thoughts on the Nature of Mass Movements*
Jane Jacobs's *The Death and Life of Great American Cities*
Robert Lucas's *Why Doesn't Capital Flow from Rich to Poor Countries?*
Jay Macleod's *Ain't No Makin' It: Aspirations and Attainment in a Low Income Neighborhood*
Elaine May's *Homeward Bound: American Families in the Cold War Era*
Douglas McGregor's *The Human Side of Enterprise*
C. Wright Mills's *The Sociological Imagination*

Thomas Piketty's *Capital in the Twenty-First Century*
Robert D. Putman's *Bowling Alone*
David Riesman's *The Lonely Crowd: A Study of the Changing American Character*
Edward Said's *Orientalism*
Joan Wallach Scott's *Gender and the Politics of History*
Theda Skocpol's *States and Social Revolutions*
Max Weber's *The Protestant Ethic and the Spirit of Capitalism*

THEOLOGY

Augustine's *Confessions*
Benedict's *Rule of St Benedict*
Gustavo Gutiérrez's *A Theology of Liberation*
Carole Hillenbrand's *The Crusades: Islamic Perspectives*
David Hume's *Dialogues Concerning Natural Religion*
Immanuel Kant's *Religion within the Boundaries of Mere Reason*
Ernst Kantorowicz's *The King's Two Bodies: A Study in Medieval Political Theology*
Søren Kierkegaard's *The Sickness Unto Death*
C. S. Lewis's *The Abolition of Man*
Saba Mahmood's *The Politics of Piety: The Islamic Revival and the Feminist Subject*
Baruch Spinoza's *Ethics*
Keith Thomas's *Religion and the Decline of Magic*

COMING SOON

Chris Argyris's *The Individual and the Organisation*
Seyla Benhabib's *The Rights of Others*
Walter Benjamin's *The Work Of Art in the Age of Mechanical Reproduction*
John Berger's *Ways of Seeing*
Pierre Bourdieu's *Outline of a Theory of Practice*
Mary Douglas's *Purity and Danger*
Roland Dworkin's *Taking Rights Seriously*
James G. March's *Exploration and Exploitation in Organisational Learning*
Ikujiro Nonaka's *A Dynamic Theory of Organizational Knowledge Creation*
Griselda Pollock's *Vision and Difference*
Amartya Sen's *Inequality Re-Examined*
Susan Sontag's *On Photography*
Yasser Tabbaa's *The Transformation of Islamic Art*
Ludwig von Mises's *Theory of Money and Credit*

Printed in the United States
by Baker & Taylor Publisher Services